Women in busines

The pivotal role of the small business in the economy was widely hailed in the west at the end of the 1980s. It has also been well accepted that women have formed a noticeable proportion of the self-employed sector. But despite this, the significance of female entrepreneurship seems to have been neglected by researchers and policy makers alike.

In this volume the work of leading researchers illustrates the multifaceted involvement of women in enterprise and self-employment. Women's businesses are examined and linked to the wider issues of the position of women in the world of work, their household and domestic responsibilities and their financial and educational training needs. The findings are consistently related back to the significance this focus has for all small business activity and research into it.

This volume makes clear that gender relations, and the ways in which they facilitate or obstruct business activity, form a crucial element in understanding the development of business in different societies. These findings will interest those social scientists and policy makers engaged in analysing the current trends that will shape the future of work and business.

Sheila Allen is a Professor of Sociology at the University of Bradford and **Carole Truman** is a Senior Lecturer in the Department of Applied Community Studies at The Manchester Metropolitan University.

Social analysis
A Series in the Social Sciences
Edited by Richard Scase, University of Kent

Beyond Class Images: Explorations in the Structure of Social Consciousness
Howard H. Davies
Fundamental Concepts and the Sociological Enterprise
C. C. Harris
Urban Planning in a Capitalist Society
Gwyneth Kirk
The State in Western Europe
Edited by Richard Scase
Autonomy and Control at the Workplace: Contexts for Job Redesign
Edited by John E. Kelly and Chris W. Clegg
The Entrepreneurial Middle Class
Richard Scase and Robert Goffee
Capitalism, the State and Industrial Relations: The Case of Britain
Dominic Strinati
Alcohol, Youth and the State
Nicholas Dorn
The Evolution of Industrial Systems
Timothy Leggatt
Sociological Interpretations of Education
David Blackledge and Barry Hunt
Sociological Approaches to Health and Medicine
Myfanwy Morgan, Michael Calnan and Nick Manning
School Organisation: A Sociological Perspective
William Tyler
Entrepreneurship in Europe
Edited by Robert Goffee and Richard Scase
The Theory and Philosophy of Organizations: Critical Issues and New Perspectives
Edited by John Hassard and Denis Pym
Small Business and Society
David Goss
Deciphering the Enterprise Culture
Roger Burrows
Paths of Enterprise
James Curran and Robert A Blackburn

Women in business
Perspectives on women entrepreneurs

Edited by Sheila Allen and
Carole Truman

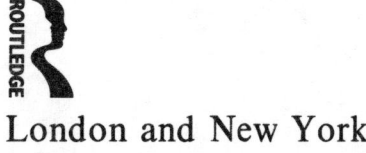

London and New York

First published 1993
by Routledge
11 New Fetter Lane, London EC4P 4EE

Simultaneously published in the USA and Canada
by Routledge
29 West 35th Street, New York, NY 10001

© 1993 Editorial matter and selection Sheila Allen and Carole Truman.

© 1993 Individual chapters to their authors.

Typeset in Times by Witwell Ltd, Southport
Printed and bound in Great Britain by
Biddles Ltd, Guildford and King's Lynn

All rights reserved. No part of this book may be reprinted
or reproduced or utilized in any form or by any electronic,
mechanical, or other means, now known or hereafter
invented, including photocopying and recording, or in any
information storage or retrieval system, without permission
in writing from the publishers.

British Library Cataloguing in Publication Data

A catalogue record for this book is available from the British Library
ISBN 0-415-063116 (hbk)   0-415-063124 (pbk)

Library of Congress Cataloging in Publication Data has been applied for

Contents

List of figure and tables vii
Notes on contributors ix
Preface xii

1 **Women and men entrepreneurs: life strategies, business strategies** 1
   Sheila Allen and Carole Truman

2 **Female petty entrepreneurs and their multiple roles** 14
   T. Scarlett Epstein

3 **Rural women** 28
   Mary Jones

4 **The minerva matrix women entrepreneurs: their perception of their management style** 46
   Nadine Vokins

5 **Women entrepreneurs and the granting of business credit** 57
   Gerda Koper

6 **Male and female entrepreneurs and their businesses: a comparative study** 70
   Steve Johnson and David Storey

7 **Business start-up training: the gender dimension** 86
   Patricia Richardson and Christina Hartshorn

8 **Not just for pin money: a case study of the West Midlands Clothing Business Start-Up Project** 101
   Davinder Kaur and Carol Hayden

9 **Good practice in business advice and counselling** 121
   Carole Truman

10	**Women's business in Europe: EEC initiatives** *Caroline Turner*	133
11	**Female business ownership: current research and possibilities for the future** *Sara Carter*	148
	Bibliography	161
	Author index	171
	Subject index	174

Figure and Tables

FIGURE

8.1 Needs of the trainees　　109

TABLES

5.1 New entrepreneurs: characteristics by desirability and sex-typing　　65
5.2 Entrepreneurs' views of their rating on the most desirable characteristics　　66
6.1 Position in firm of owner/manager by gender　　74
6.2 Sectoral distribution of sample by gender of owner/manager　　74
6.3 Date of firm start-up by gender of founder – retail, catering and other services　　75
6.4 Age of founder at time of start-up by gender of founder – retail, catering and other services　　75
6.5 Characteristics of new firm founders by gender – retail, catering and other services　　77
6.6 Sources of start-up finance by gender of founder – retail, catering and other services　　77
6.7 Problems faced in first year by gender of founder – retail, catering and other services　　78
6.8 Annual turnover in 1984 by gender of owner/manager – retail, catering and other services　　78
6.9 Profitability in 1985 by gender of owner/manager – retail, catering and other services　　79
6.10 Number of employees (including owner) by gender of owner/manager – retail, catering and other services　　79

viii *Women in business*

6.11	Composition of workforce in 1985 by gender of owner/manager – retail, catering and other services	80
6.12	Change in volume of turnover 1982–4 by gender of owner/manager – retail, catering and other services	81
6.13	Introduction of new technology 1982–5 by gender of owner/manager – retail, catering and other services	81
6.14	Employment change 1982–5 by gender of owner/manager – retail, catering and other services	82
6.15	Position of firm in 1988 by gender of owner/manager – retail, catering and other services	82
6.16	Changes in turnover and profitability 1984–5 by gender of owner/manager – retail, catering and other services	83
6.17	Employment change 1985–7 by gender of owner/manager – retail, catering and other services	84
7.1	Percentage increase in self-employed by sex 1979–88 – Great Britain	88
7.2	Self-employment by sex, 1979–88 – United Kingdom	88
7.3	Female self-employment as a percentage of total self-employment – regional analysis 1989	89
7.4	Some examples of the assistance available for business start-up	92
8.1	Clients by race and gender 1988–9	104
8.2	Initial employment status by race – female clients	105
8.3	Initial employment status by race – male clients	106
8.4	Proportions of different client groups attending business skills courses	110
8.5	Progress of clients 1988–9 as at June 1989	113
8.6	Trading businesses as at June 1989 by race and gender (numbers and percentage of each client group)	114

Contributors

Sheila Allen is Professor of Sociology at the University of Bradford. Her current research includes a study of women running their own businesses, women and social change in mining communities, and self-employment and disability. She has researched and published extensively on work and employment, race relations and gender.

Sara Carter is currently a lecturer at the Scottish Enterprise Foundation, University of Stirling, where she has spent several years researching and writing on the topic of business ownership. Her latest book (with Tom Cannon) is *Enterprising Women* (Academic Press 1991).

Christina Hartshorn is Enterprise Officer for Women in Scotland and Lecturer, Scottish Enterprise Foundation, University of Stirling. She was awarded a German Marshall Foundation Fellowship in 1987 to visit and review innovative enterprise provision for women in the USA. Her interests lie in women's business creation and management development for women.

Carol Hayden is Principal Economic Development Officer at Coventry City Council. While employed as Senior Economist at the West Midlands Enterprise Board she was responsible for establishing the Clothing Business Start-Up Project. Since 1983 she has been active in developing work on clothing industry strategy and women's employment initiatives in the West Midlands.

Steve Johnson is Projects Manager of the Policy Research Unit at Leeds Polytechnic and an Associate Fellow of the Institute for Employment Research at the University of Warwick. He has researched and written widely in the areas of small business economics, self-employment and local economic development. His current research interests include local skills surveys, training policy and policies for small business growth.

x Women in business

Mary Jones was formerly Lecturer in Business Studies, specializing in accounting and finance. She studied part-time for a Degree in Business Studies and a Diploma in Marketing and was a full-time student on the MBA Programme at the University of Warwick 1990/91. She has researched and presented papers, and published on women entrepreneurs.

Davinder Kaur is Business Consultant at the West Midlands Clothing Resource Centre, where she has managed the Clothing Business Start-Up Project since its establishment. Previously she was employed in the clothing industry, concentrating on export and marketing throughout Western Europe.

Gerda Koper was a former research assistant at the Department of Social and Organizational Psychology, University of Leiden, The Netherlands. Her main interest was in the field of social justice and, in particular, procedural justice. In June 1991 she started her own Sport Consultancy and Research bureau and at present is a manager at a large sports centre and does research on sports motivation.

Patricia Richardson is a lecturer in small business with the Scottish Enterprise Foundation, University of Stirling. She has researched the impact of government policy on small firms in inner city areas and has been involved in the design and implementation of practical support for small businesses. Her interests lie in women's business creation and the generation of business ideas.

T. Scarlett Epstein qualified as a development economist and development anthropologist. She has spent many years researching and consulting on the socio-economic aspects of Third World development. Having published widely on this subject she edits a series of books under the heading 'Women in Development'. A former Research Professor at the University of Sussex, she is now Director of SESAC (Scarlett Epstein Social Assessment Consultancy) and Innovative Development Research; she also organizes the secretariat for the International Committee for Development Market Research.

David Storey is Director of Research at the Centre for Small and Medium Sized Enterprises at the University of Warwick. His main research interests are in entrepreneurship, small firm growth and failure, and managerial labour markets. He is the author or co-author of several books and articles including *Entrepreneurship and the Small Firm* (1982), *Job Generation and Labour Market Change* (1987) and *The Performance of Small Firms* (1987). He is currently national co-ordinator of the Economic and Social Research Council Small Business Initiative.

Carole Truman is a Senior Lecturer in Social Policy at Manchester Metropolitan University. She was formerly employed as Research Fellow at Bradford University where she undertook a study of Women's Experiences of Small Business. She has also researched and written on Equal Opportunities and aspects of women's paid and unpaid work. Her present research involves looking at the needs of the elderly and their carers in the community. She is also interested in exploring the methods and processes of social research from the perspectives of equal opportunities/anti-discrimination.

Caroline Turner read Social Anthropology and Economics and Marketing at the University of London. Resident in Greece since 1982, she is a researcher and consultant on women's enterprise creation to institutions both in Greece and elsewhere. She is European Coordinator for and represents Greece on the EC Commission Network on Women in Local Employment Initiatives. Her particular fields of interest are small and medium sized enterprises, women's employment and enterprise creation, and local government.

Nadine Vokins studied at Oxford University. She is presently Senior Lecturer in Communication and Interpersonal Skills at Bristol Business School, Bristol Polytechnic. Her interests include tourism, international links and cultural differences, women's management issues, and poetry.

Preface

This book originated in a weekend conference which took place in May 1989 at the University of Bradford. The 'Women Entrepreneurs' conference was organized by Sheila Allen and Carole Truman as part of their work in the Work and Gender Research Unit in the Department of Social and Economic Studies, and by Women in Enterprise, whose Director Ms Kaye Smith gave invaluable help, as did her colleague Ms Marjorie Povall.

The chapters in this book represent a selection of the papers given at the conference. Over seventy participants contributed to the proceedings and we should like to thank all those who gave papers, chaired the plenary and workshop sessions and the many others, who engaged in the very lively discussions which were a marked feature of the whole conference. The participants included researchers on entrepreneurship among women, those from a range of public and private agencies which give information and advice on all aspects of business enterprise, and others from networks, groups and organizations of women, who run or intend to start-up their own businesses, some of whom came from networks and organizations of black and ethnic minority women. The majority were located in Britain. There was also a strong presence of women from several member states of the European Community.

Our thanks are due to the Equal Opportunities Unit of the EC, the Equal Opportunities Commission and the Department of Employment for their assistance and financial support which enabled the conference to bring together so many concerned with women entrepreneurs. Mary Jones read the whole of an earlier draft of the book and her help was much appreciated.

We are grateful, as always, to Mrs Win Healey who has with her unfailing competence and good humour worked with us to produce this volume.

Sheila Allen
Work and Gender Research Unit
University of Bradford

Carole Truman
Department of Applied Community Studies
The Manchester Metropolitan University

1 Women and men entrepreneurs
Life strategies, business strategies

Sheila Allen and Carole Truman

John Major, subsequently to become the Prime Minister of Britain, was reported as saying in May 1989 when he was Chief Secretary to the Treasury that 'There is a great deal of evidence to show that the jobs and products of tomorrow are highly likely to come from the activities of the small business sector . . . in our judgment the future belongs to them' (quoted in Leighton and Felstead 1992: 15). Such opinions about the increasingly pivotal role of small businesses were common during the 1980s, from government and politicians, from some business quarters and from some academics, not only in Britain and the European Community, but in the United States and the Pacific Rim countries. And recently they have featured as part of the Eastern European discourses on moves to market economies. In this sense it can be said that there was in the space of a decade an ideological change, probably most marked in Britain, from regarding the term entrepreneur as one of mild abuse (Hobbs 1991) to seeing enterprise as central to regenerating a declining economy. How far a culture of enterprise became embedded, beyond the widespread use of the term, is much more open to question.

This book focuses on one dimension of business enterprise – that of the salience of women's experience. The issues this raises for a broader and more adequate understanding of business activity are discussed in this chapter. As will become clear, not only women but also the gender dimension are still areas very much neglected in research on business enterprise and much basic information is lacking. From a social scientific perspective we would argue that an understanding of the processes and practices of gender relations, and how far these facilitate or obstruct business activity, is a crucial element in understanding the development and prospects for success and failure of such activity. Here we might note that in many areas of research and policy making gender divisions are neglected, resulting in a variety of consequences,

2 *Women in business*

both for social scientific research and for effective policy implementation. For instance, the ignoring by development aid programmes and in official statistics of the vital role of women in food production (in many parts of Africa some estimate that 80 per cent of food is produced by women) is a major contributory factor to malnutrition and starvation (see Epstein this volume).[1] We are faced with fragmented evidence about the social processes and practices which constrain (or facilitate) women in their entrepreneurial endeavours. This lack of evidence raises questions which deserve close attention by policy makers, financial agencies, trainers, equal opportunities units and, of course, politicians whether they adopt the entrepreneurial ethos or not. Women are subjected to ideologies about their 'place' and their obligations to the household and family and these affect perceptions of their economic activity, some of which is recorded and recognized, much of which is not. Official statistics fail to record their contribution in the formal sector as 'helpers' or 'unpaid' workers, and appear to be unable to record them with any reliability as self-employed and business owners. This problem is world-wide and has been labelled as 'statistical' purdah.[2]

CLASSIFYING BUSINESS ENTERPRISE

Rapid increases in self-employment and the number of businesses registered were regularly referred to in the 1980s, both in Britain and across Europe. Taking the statistical records of the European Community at face value, there is considerable variation between the twelve member states for the period 1986–89 in the proportion of the labour force categorized as self-employed. The overall increase for the same period was 0.3 per cent. Looking at the decade 1979–89 for what was then ten member states, the increase was near to 10 per cent, with the UK almost doubling from 7.4 to 13.4 per cent of the labour force, Italy increasing 1.9, Belgium +1.5 and Germany +0.3. The other states all decreased, Greece -3.9, Denmark -3.6, Luxembourg -1.7, Ireland -0.9, the Netherlands -0.2, except France which showed slight increases in the middle of the decade but ended as it begun with 12.5 per cent of its workforce defined as self-employed (Eurostat Labour Force Surveys).

The problems associated with using statistics across member states (and elsewhere) and within them to establish comparisons of the proportion of the self-employed and rates of growth and decline have been widely discussed (Allen and Truman 1992; Allen and Wolkowitz 1987; Casey and Creigh 1988; Loutfi 1992). Here we simply raise those most relevant to the concerns of this book.

Eurostat estimates are based on figures supplied by member states. Taking the UK as an example, variations of up to 10 per cent are recorded depending on whether or not owner-managers of incorporated businesses are included as self-employed; also, data from official sample surveys regularly show differences of several per cent in the proportions of self-employed, between the General Household Survey (GHS) and the Labour Force Survey (LFS). These differences arise from a number of technical decisions about who should be included and excluded, and where self-reporting is involved there are reasons (including tax and social security regulations) which are thought to affect responses. Unpaid family workers are included in the International Labour Office statistics, but not in those of several member states. The wording of questions can be crucial to whether or not responses bring into the figures categories such as working (unpaid) spouses, usually women. In 1987, for example, an additional 10 million women, either non-salaried but working in a partner's business, or earning an income as self-employed, increased the total of women officially recorded among the self-employed in the EC from 3.2 million to 12.5 million (EEC 1987). Such problems are not simply technical ones, but display the gender bias which characterises the concepts of work, including self-employment, which are used in official estimates (Allen and Truman 1992).

The small firm figures prominently in the discussions of economic regeneration and the enterprise culture. The definition of 'small' has been based on a number of different conventions rather than on sociological conceptions of social interaction, social and moral density or primary groupings. There are obvious sociological differences between a family and a firm, and the question 'what do we find when the family is the firm?' has rarely been asked in research on business enterprise and, with the exception of work on self-employed or business women, has even more rarely been investigated. This example is dealt with, though usually obliquely, in some chapters in this book and is important when considering the conventional definitions. The most usual definition of small is a firm with up to 200 employees, medium is from 200 to 499 employees, and large indicates more than 500 employees. Within the small category some states in Europe collect information on micro-business, i.e. those with 0 to 9 employees. It has been pointed out that in terms of numbers of companies registered these micro-businesses account for most of the growth that occurred in the 1980s (Leighton and Felstead 1992). The discussion of business activity in many of the following chapters relates to micro-business. Size in terms of numbers of employees is not the only factor which has to be considered. In terms of work relationships, management styles, decision making, working conditions and hours, and values and practices, many other factors have to be taken into account if we are to understand the success or failure of, and the obstacles or opportunities offered by small business and its role in the economy.

ANALYSING SOCIAL AND ECONOMIC CHANGE

Social scientists are properly concerned with several levels of enquiry. These range from descriptive accounts through to analyses which situate descriptive data within theoretical frameworks drawn from one or more disciplines. There are many differences within and between these disciplines but the objective in general is to understand and explain the processes and structures of social phenomena. Some social scientists adopt some of the approaches and procedures of natural scientists dealing with physical phenomena, and biologists and medical scientists who attempt to explain, predict and prescribe for the areas they have marked out as their preserve.

The need to understand the meanings people ascribe to their own actions and the behaviour of others is stressed particularly by sociologists concerned to avoid an over-determined structural model. The relation of human agency to social process and structure is never a simple matter and voluntaristic theories of enterprise, while they have a place, are not sufficient to explain the restructuring of economies and within that the varying patterns of behaviour and action labelled as enterprise.

The contributors to this book adopt a variety of approaches to and positions on the agency–structure relationship. For the most part their studies are located in largely uncharted territory as they consider the experiences and role of women and occasionally of gender in the 1980s small business world.

It has to be remembered that social science remains 'a poor relation' massively under-resourced, in comparison with the physical sciences, and is not culturally accepted as 'real' science; it remains on the margins of the 'scientific' discourse and few listen to its research findings. This is particularly the case in Britain, compared both to the United States and the European Community. The British Government appears singularly unable to take the research findings on enterprise and entrepreneurship seriously, despite its rhetoric about self-employment, small business enterprise and the employment potential of this sector.

Where does a social scientist begin to deal with the many issues raised by enterprise and entrepreneurship, especially if they are to take account of the social divisions of gender? The first task, it can be argued, is to situate entrepreneurship in its historical perspective. The received wisdom of the developments in the nineteenth century or even earlier in England, portrays the entrepreneur as a self-made man, a paternalist employer working initially beside his employees and becoming a captain of industry, through his own enterprise and hard work. However inaccurate such a portrayal may be when tested against historical realities, and this is particularly the case when the histories take account of the contribution of women and children to the image of the 'self-made man', new life was breathed into it during the 1980s.

The second task is to explore the development of markets for labour throughout the twentieth century. Whatever the current ideology and reality about self-employment and business enterprise as mainstream economic activities, they were for most of this period on the margins of economic development.

The third task is to examine the influence of the 'entrepreneurial' ideology of the 1980s, which became pervasive in sectors of the polity as well as the economy. Many information and advice centres emerged to stimulate the 'enterprise' economy (Truman 1989). There were many who, with or without such help, embarked on the search for self-employment or owning their own business. Was this the result of the enterprise culture or of economic restructuring combined with a lack of other employment opportunities?

From the late 1970s in Britain and other advanced industrial societies, changes in the polity and economy have been variously characterized as processes of restructuring, a decline in corporatist and collective production and a growth in individual enterprise. The increase in self-employment and small businesses was heralded not only as a panacea for economic ills, as part of a more *laissez-faire*, deregulated and privatized market for goods and services, but also as constituting a regeneration of values and practices associated with the freedom to work for oneself, and to emerge from a dependency on the state, from public sector industries as well as from welfare provisions.

It is not surprising that social scientists have been unable to provide a synoptic theory to encompass the social, political and economic changes or even to give an adequate description of all the facets of restructuring and their consequences for the everyday lives of men and women. Communities formerly dependent on primary production such as coal mining, or on manufacturing such as textiles, steel or shipbuilding, at least as far as the male labour force was concerned, saw a decline in the demand for labour. 'Real' jobs, defined largely as those done by men on a full-time, regular, permanent basis became ever more scarce, and work in the service sector, which had provided alternative openings for men and even more for part-time women, began to decline. As the decade progressed a social science literature developed to account for these changes and to assess the extent to which small-scale enterprise was filling the gaps left by the recession, and more broadly how far petty production could be said to be more central to the economy than it had been for many decades. Disentangling the ideology of the enterprise culture from the reality of growing economic insecurity for large sectors of the population through deindustrialization has not proved to be an easy task (Poland 1992).

During the 1970s and the 1980s there was a considerable shift in the approaches to the sociology of work and labour markets. One major aspect of this shift was the reformulation of work to include economic activities beyond those of employment. Some of this rethinking was associated with attempts to explain labour markets and income-generating work in the Third World and derived from a concern with the neglect of women's work (both paid and unpaid) in industrialized and developing economies (Bromley and Gerry 1979; Davies 1979; Elson and Pearson 1989: Jenson et al. 1988; MacEwen Scott 1979; Pahl 1988; Redclift and Mingione 1985). During the late 1970s up until the mid 1980s a discourse on 'the future of work' mingled speculation about new domestic forms of production in which the family would evolve into a 'new work collective' through a growth of home-based work in the 'electronic household' (Toffler 1980) with attempts to point to the family as a self-provisioning unit using their own privately owned tools and machinery to make and maintain household necessities and to exchange goods and services with other households, outside the cash nexus (Gershuny 1979, 1985; Gershuny and Pahl 1979/80). For a critical discussion of this discourse see Allen and Wolkowitz (1987).

Underlying many of the attempts to account for the rise of small enterprises is the more general question of petty commodity production and income generating work, and their relation to multinational capitalist organization. This takes many forms.

It has been argued that the profound changes involved in the restructuring during the 1980s required 'an appropriate "cultural" management' and this was supplied by the enterprise culture discourse, stressing individualistic solutions to structural problems (Burrows and Curran 1991: 12). The independent small scale business competing with others, using flexible labour, self-help and private capital was seen as the answer to many of Britain's economic and social problems. A new and more central role was given, within this discourse, to small scale enterprise which had for decades been theorized as peripheral to large scale corporatist economic organization. The arguments were frequently couched in terms of post-Fordism (Atkinson 1984a and b; Boyer 1987, 1988; Sabel 1982). These projected a new economic structure characterized by 'flexible specialization' and a fragmentation of markets which were best served by small units of production, based on local networks, in which new technologies and the revival of crafts were married to provide income and work on the one hand and to meet the needs of the market on the other. Though small and local or regional in nature these enterprises were seen as part of a new international division of labour. Through them, specialization and rapid responses to changes in demand could by the use of new technology overcome the problems of distance and serve international markets, not only in industrialized societies, but in the Third World.

These arguments have been criticized on several grounds (Pollert 1988, 1991). One is that the small scale business, particularly in manufacturing, lacks independence from large scale economic organizations. Rainnie (1989, 1990) illustrated this by his study of the clothing industry and Allen and Wolkowitz (1987) argued that the widespread use of homeworking labour in both manufacturing and service industries, while not a new economic formation, was integral to economic restructuring and large scale operations. A further argument has been that the growth of small scale economic activities in the 1980s was recession-induced in Britain and not the sign of economic regeneration (Brown and Scase 1991; Gerry 1985). Fevre (1986) illustrates the development of sub-contracting in the steel industry and Schutt and Whittington (1984) discuss the out-sourcing of production. Privatization and deregulation facilitated new enterprises in printing, transport, security services, cleaning in schools and hospitals and more recently in the upkeep of royal and public parks.

It was in this context that research on small business enterprise was developed in the 1980s (Burrows and Curran 1991). We have discussed these developments elsewhere and we note here only that for those who had already researched gender relations within a wider perspective of labour markets and household divisions of labour, along with other dimensions of gendered social relations, the frameworks adopted in small business research appeared inappropriate to deal with the realities of the everyday circumstances and experiences of self-employed women and business owners (Allen et al. 1992; Daune-Richard 1988).

It was from this background that we initiated the conference on women entrepreneurs. We were a few months into a research project on Women in Business Enterprise and were already aware of the number and range of organizations, networks and groups focused on women in business and self-employment.[3] It was clear that there had been too little research on women entrepreneurs, too little attention paid to the obstacles which confront women starting up in business and the factors making for success or failure. There was, however, a range of unsubstantiated claims about the characteristics women entrepreneurs exhibit as individuals and about how they are expected to behave in relation to men and dependants, especially children. These and other issues are taken up in the following chapters.

RESEARCHING WOMEN'S ENTERPRISE

These chapters serve to highlight various themes and issues which have been the focus of investigation into women's entrepreneurship. The authors come from a range of academic disciplines and professional interests. This diversity reflects a range of agendas where women's entrepreneurship may be raised. The chapters point to many commonalities amongst women business owners: the difficulties of access to capital and credit, domestic responsibilities and access to technical know-how are examples.

These areas are central to our understanding of women's involvement in small business. The importance of access to credit is identified as a major barrier to entry into self-employment throughout the world. For women who have no other source of income petty trading may begin with only a few pence of financial investment. The most significant investment these women make is their labour input and high levels of efficiency which are essential to reduce risks in their economic activity. Restricted access to capital and collateral remains a key barrier to women achieving financial security within their entrepreneurial activity.

A further constraint on women's business activity is that of sectoral segregation. Several contributors focus on gender-specific divisions of labour which restrict the areas in which women operate. Throughout the world women are most likely to be found in food production, nutrition, health and child care. This segregation is compounded by lack of access to technical know-how to enable them to operate in other markets.

A feature stressed in most contributions is the need to address women's business involvement in the context of other facets of their lives. Several authors show how constraints on time and spatial mobility as a result of household and domestic responsibilities impose further restrictions. For women, managing a business and managing household responsibilities are integrated in such a way that one is intrinsic to the other. It cannot be assumed, however, that their decisions about business activity are always subordinate to family and household responsibilities.

The chapter by Epstein on women in the Third World contains obvious comparisons with Jones' findings on women located in a rural area of Britain. Both demonstrate the centrality of self-employment in women's life strategies. Epstein also discusses the way in which policy makers and planners fail to recognize and respond to woman-headed households despite the dominance of women traders in many African states. Seventy per cent of rural women in Kenya are in trade and 50 per cent sell their own produce. Estimates suggest that between 50 and 90 per cent of women in West Africa engage in some form of trading such as their involvement in farm and marine produce or non-exploitative food processing work.

Jones describes women's prevalence in income generation and entrepreneurial activity. Her study set in rural Shropshire identifies the importance of a family tradition in self-employment. The breadth of women's roles in supporting families and businesses provides considerable scope for further investigation and more accurate recording, as discussed earlier in this chapter. The use of women's time and time management were among the biggest problems articulated by the women Jones interviewed. It is clear that underpinning this is the potential for self-exploitation within entrepreneurship, where the boundaries between paid and unpaid work are diffuse and obscure.

The internal dynamics of well-established and successful women's businesses are explored by Vokins. Her interest is with the way that women operate their businesses and how they perceive themselves as managers. What emerges is a clear sense of the values incorporated into how women manage their businesses, particularly in the initial stages. There are also tensions as competing and contradictory values and styles associated with the development of businesses are experienced. Ultimately, Vokins' study provides a sound argument for broadening the criteria which are used to judge 'good' managers and the scope and curricula of management or small business courses. The socio-psychological perspective on women's business activity is continued by Koper, who explores the social interaction between banks and entrepreneurs in The Netherlands. The investigation included both men and women and draws out comparisons between them. She provides evidence to show how the procedures used by banks for granting credit, including the sex-role perceptions of bank employees, discriminate against women. Koper's chapter exposes a common problem for women entrepreneurs, and using an affirmative action approach she outlines the action government and financial institutions must take to remove such barriers.

Johnson and Storey analyse the quantitative data from two surveys conducted in 1985 and 1988 in six labour market areas to demonstrate the 'demographic profile' and performance of men's and women's businesses. They make direct comparisons between male and female business owners. Their data suggest that using the measures selected, there are more similarities than differences between female and male businesses. This is not altogether surprising since some of the processes of owning and operating a small business must span some of the social and economic divisions between men and women. What they were unable to investigate was how many women and men had been unable to start a business because of the failure to obtain finance. Several interesting findings emerge which demonstrate the advantages of comparative work on gender in small business research. Additionally, the questions they were unable to answer point towards the kind of research needed if we are to understand and explain the salience of gender.

The next four chapters deal with various aspects of agencies and networks available to those who run small businesses or are self-employed, and those who are considering taking such a step. The agencies, like the management courses discussed by Vokins and the banks investigated by Koper, are in general geared to the perceived needs of men. Richardson and Hartshorn explore in some detail the process of small business start-up and in particular the training available to new entrepreneurs. In common with other chapters which illustrate that for women, self-employment is a life strategy as much as it is a business strategy, Richardson and Hartshorn point to the need for training and support to be organized at times and with the facilities which make them available to women. Although they emphasize the need for the development of personal as well as technical and business skills, they argue that training courses should be held away from domestic environments and child care responsibilities in order to allow the time and space for the women to re-assess realistically their existing obligations and the taking on of new ones. This separation between home lives and personal development, whether in education, training, setting up a business or organizing collectively is a frequently made observation on and by women. It reflects the different meanings

Life strategies, business strategies 11

and realities of home environments for men and women based on the structured inequalities of the domestic division of labour. Such a separation is a basic tenet of the Self-Employed Women's Association, a highly successful, multifaceted women's organization in India (Ela Bhatt, personal communication).

A further example of a small business support network is discussed by Kaur and Hayden in their account of a project within a resource centre for those entering self-employment in the West Midlands clothing industry. One of the main aims of the project was to maximize the employment potential of small businesses. The project became a core part of the work of the centre and was open to men and women disadvantaged in employment. The clients were predominantly from inner city areas and included people of Afro-Caribbean and Asian origin and descent, as well as white individuals, though not in proportion to their presence in the clothing industry. The authors' approach stresses the need to avoid making problems of particular groups of women, and their potential to succeed in business; in other words, the need to avoid stereotyping. They point out that starting a small business, especially in a highly competetive market, is neither glamorous nor easy for anyone, and that each person who makes the attempt faces problems which need to be overcome. The crucial element appears to be an ongoing support network, such as the project, that provides professional help and advice staffed by those with the knowledge and skills relevant to the industry, from sources of raw materials through to its markets. Clearly, lessons can be learned of a practical nature from this case study, but also the analysis of gender, race and age is integrated with features of the industry, region and market in a way which gives it a depth lacking in much small business research. Through this case we learn what can (and cannot) be done.

Truman discusses ways in which many business support advice agencies have failed to take on board women's perspectives in starting up and running businesses and so the service which they offer may not be in tune with women's needs. She outlines proposals by which they can adapt their generic advice network to encompass the lifestyles and perspectives common to many women's lives and business experience. Turner broadens this discussion to explore European initiatives which have been developed to provide support for women's business activity. She outlines similarities and differences in women's business activity in member states of the European Community. She demonstrates considerable disparities between the types and availability of support for different forms of women's business activity. However, as Turner concludes, very little has been done to evaluate the effectiveness of such initiatives, either from the point of view of whether money has been well spent, or whether initiatives have been adequately tailored to provide support where women need it most.

In the final chapter, Carter contextualizes some of the earlier research on female business ownership and argues for the need to explore new research questions, adopting new methodologies within interdisciplinary frameworks. She points to the lack of coherent conceptual frameworks in earlier research and discusses the methodological problems of investigating key questions on women's business activity.

In this chapter we have argued that theoretically and practically our understanding of women's involvement in the small business sector remains sparse. The other chapters raise many issues crucial to this understanding, and in some cases to the similarities and differences between business men and business women. However, as our earlier discussion indicates many questions have not been asked. This is due in large part to the structuring of gender relations, materially and ideologically, both in social science conceptions of the everyday world and in that world itself. There are, for instance, some data on self-employed and business women's lack of autonomy, because of their domestic/family responsibilities rather than the demands of their business activity. We do not know, however, about businessmen with regard to their non-business responsibilities; they are presumed to have wives and families, who are frequently assumed to provide free labour and skills. Their lack of autonomy is discussed only in terms of the demands of their businesses. Clearly these gendered assumptions and presumptions need investigation in comparative work on women and men. In terms of self-exploitation, a propensity assumed in many studies of self-employment and the initial stages of business start-up, some information exists, but studies comparing men and women are lacking. Is the degree of self-exploitation the same? What degree of choice do men and women have? What factors restrict their choices?

We have discussed elsewhere the impact of life cycle stages on women and their business activity (Allen and Truman 1992), but their relevance to men remains unresearched. Though self-employment is frequently put forward as an option following redundancy, is it also increasingly turned to much earlier by those never employed, as Kaur and Hayden (Chapter 8) propose?

With record numbers of business failures in the early 1990s it becomes even more important that both men's and women's experiences of obtaining credit be more fully researched. If, as much research so far indicates, women find it much harder to get credit to start-up businesses than men (though as consumers women are heavily targeted by banks and finance houses as well as retailers of all kinds to buy on credit), can this be because of their initial lack of access to collateral? Men are more likely to be able to use their homes as collateral, with the risk of losing it if the business fails. Although the behaviour of banks and financial institutions towards men and women may differ on grounds of sexist assumptions, for those who do obtain credit the financial markets may be much more important than gender in explaining business success or failure.

The role of small business and self-employment in the capitalist market economies of the last decade of the twentieth century can only be understood through an historical grounding of the concepts and an integration of wider sets of social relations, including gender, age, ethnicity, race and class into the analyses of these economic activities.

NOTES

1 See Pietilä and Vickers (1990: 14–19) for a discussion of 'the totally false picture' of women's work in agriculture given by ordinary national and international statistics, and the failure of many agricultural and rural development programmes as a consequence.
2 A census in Pakistan recorded 147 women as egg and poultry producers, a task regularly allotted to and performed by women not only there, but in rural areas everywhere (Shirley Nuss, personal communication).
3 We wish to acknowledge a grant from The Leverhulme Trust for our research project Women in Business Enterprise.

2 Female petty entrepreneurs and their multiple roles[1]

T. Scarlett Epstein

Women perform an important role in the building of the real back bone of the nation's economy, the small and medium-scale enterprises, as well as the cottage industries.

Sanvictores

This chapter focuses on the distinct features and roles of Third World female entrepreneurs. It begins with an outline of the different types of entrepreneurial activities pursued by rural women, and by using case studies it illustrates how women succeed as petty entrepreneurs whilst operating within an extremely difficult socio-economic environment. The argument continues by exploring why rural women are generally restricted to petty entrepreneurship and what prevents them from organizing and/or managing larger ventures. The final section concentrates on some of the measures necessary to enable more rural women to realize their entrepreneurial potential on a larger scale.

Poverty accompanied by lack of income-earning opportunities, rather than profit incentives, motivates an increasing number of rural women to become petty entrepreneurs. These women are thus pushed out of their conventional setting rather than pulled into entrepreneurship because of the profit it offers.

The main factors which motivate rural women to become petty entrepreneurs are insufficient land to ensure a livelihood for their families and/or a lack of employment opportunities.

RURAL WOMEN AND THEIR MULTIPLE ROLES

Many studies of the role of women in rural development indicate that specialization is a luxury only the better-off can afford (see, for example, Nelson 1979). Survival strategies demand that the poorer rural women perform a multiplicity of roles. Almost invariably women are everywhere responsible for their households and child care. The lack of appropriate domestic technologies for Third World rural households makes domestic chores (including collecting firewood and water, often across long distances) extremely labour and time-consuming. In addition to performing most of the domestic duties, the majority of rural women also either work on their own farms and/or as employed labourers for larger local landowners. They act as petty entrepreneurs in addition to all these other responsibilities.

The multiple roles rural women perform and the priority their cultures give to their familial responsibilities put severe constraints not only on the radius within which they can function but also on the kinds of entrepreneurial activity they can perform.

TYPES OF FEMALE ENTERPRENEURSHIP

Evidence confirms that female petty entrepreneurs succeed in extremely competitive situations to carve out a personal niche for their respective activities.

Trade offers a welcome income-earning opportunity for many rural women. It enables them to operate at different levels of activity best suited to their specific circumstances, and it does not require large amounts of capital or a lot of skill training. Moreover, it hardly conflicts with child care responsibilities, as the presence of many infants in Third World markets shows. Trade is thus an attractive proposition for potential female entrepreneurs.

The 'higglers' of Jamaica are perhaps the prototype of small-scale itinerant peddlers who often have a part-time engagement in farming as well as urban ties. Higglering, with its roots in slavery, continued and diversified after emancipation. It represents a response to a situation of high unemployment among women and the lack of alternative occupations. By collecting supplies from remote and relatively inaccessible rural areas higglers provide an essential link between small farmers and the market place. 'They pay good prices at the farm gate and will, if necessary, after agreeing a price with the farmer reap the crop themselves, thus substituting labour for capital' (Knight and Taylor 1985: 9). Lack of credit is one of the major recurring problems higglers face. To overcome their shortage of funds,

> they often take part in a 'partner' operation in which each member passes to a 'banker' a certain amount each week, and collects a lump sum of all the input at one time in an order agreed by them. . . . Partners are usually used to obtain sufficient funding to keep up or

increase the trade. . . . It may well be necessary to form a vendor's bank as was done in the Philippines to solve the higglers' credit problem.

(Knight and Taylor 1985: 14)

Lack of foreign currency in the 1970s provided an opportunity for some of the enterprising higglers to branch out into exports and imports. While shopkeepers from the formal private sector were unable to purchase imports, the informal sector higglers found ways around the foreign exchange shortage by carrying loads of thyme and other produce to Panama, Haiti or Miami and with the proceeds of their sales they purchased goods and took them back into Jamaica.

Their aggressive public behaviour at the airports as they jostled with pleasure and business travellers to get their goods through customs and their 'capturing' of streets and sidewalks to display their goods, did not endear them to the public at large, particularly to the established merchants, who saw them as posing a threat, as they took away patronage from them. . . . However, in the confrontations between the higglers and the authorities, the higglers have emerged as a force to be reckoned with.

(Knight and Taylor 1985: 3)

All the relevant data seem to suggest that more and more women, particularly younger ones whose increasing numbers fail to be absorbed in formal sector employment, will become higglers. Therefore, the number of Jamaican higglers will grow rather than decline.

In other Third World countries rural women are also actively involved in petty trade. Mintz, for instance, reports that for Haiti 'nearly all rural women have some trading experience and were traders at one time or another in their lives' (1964: 260). Similarly,

in West Africa, it has been estimated that women traders handle 60 to 90 per cent of the domestic farm and marine produce. . . . Case studies of rural women in Kenya show that around 70 per cent of peasant women are involved in trade and some 50 per cent market their own crops. In general, women have been quick to respond to the opportunities created by growing urban demand for their produce.

(Food and Agriculture Organization undated: 4)

The same phenomenon has been reported for Indonesia (Bangun 1985), the Philippines (Castillo 1976), Papua New Guinea (Epstein 1982) and elsewhere.

The level of marketing at which these rural women operate varies

Female petty entrepreneurs 17

according to the goods traded, the services they perform and how much capital they have available. As already mentioned in the context of Jamaica, the shortage of capital and alternative employment opportunities in a setting with abundant labour often results in extreme substitution by labour for capital. Altogether, labour substitution for capital is most dramatically revealed in the distributive sector:

> The sudden acquisition of small amounts of capital which are available only for short periods of time, as sometimes occurs, can evoke an enormous investment of labour on the part of the temporary holder, anxious to show a profit before the capital must be returned to its owner.
>
> (Mintz 1964: 264)

This willingness of market women to render service often at extremely low cost ensures a high level of marketing efficiency, in spite of the usually low level of auxiliary market services, such as transport, communication, and storage, over which they have no control. A network of long term trade links between market women and their clients and/or suppliers, though it involves not only lowering the price charged or raising the price paid but also the rendering of gifts and special services, is generally welcomed by female petty traders. They are prepared to accept lower returns and/or increase their labour input to reduce the risk in their transactions. In the uncertain environment of their market trade *formalized trade* links secure a patterning and regularity without which these petty entrepreneurs understandably fear chaotic market conditions would prevail.

Business histories of female petty traders, for instance in Haiti, show that a large number started their marketing as young girls with the local currency equivalent of no more than a few pence, and a surprisingly large proportion of them managed to accumulate working capital of over £200 after some years of trading (Mintz 1964: 260). Other examples of successful female petty entrepreneurs are reported by Metraux for the Merbial Valley (Haiti) where there are:

> a large number of young girls or women who take up their stand along roads or paths, in a hut or at the foot of a tree, to sell thread, matches, candies, fruit, vegetables, cereals, spices and tobacco. Mangoes, caimitoes or avocados are arranged in little heaps, for each of which there is a fixed price. Coffee, and beans in pod, are also sold by heaps. The women who sell cola, 'clairin', candies and biscuits are constantly on the move. They go to any place in the

valley where for any reason a group of people are gathered together – for a service, a marriage, a political meeting etc.

(cited in Mintz 1964: 268)

Likewise, Vunapope market in Papua New Guinea exemplifies a spontaneous response to demand perceived by some enterprising women sellers outside the Vunapope Catholic Mission hospital to supply the needs of patients as well as of hospital staff and visitors (Epstein 1982: 17): 'Many of the vendors are maternity patients awaiting or recovering from delivery. Husbands bring a load of food for their wives, and the wives use some for immediate consumption, and some for sale, saving the money received for later purchases' (Salisbury 1970: 100).

Sales in heaps or bundles, each of which is offered at a unit price or a multiple thereof, predominate in many Third World market places. In Melanesia, for instance, price variations are expressed in terms of different quantities sold per unit of money, rather than by way of different amounts of money charged for the same quantity of goods (Epstein 1982: 12). In Mexico too 'instead of offering a fixed "package" at a variable price, the "package" is variable at a fixed price' (Cassidy 1974: 49). This is reflected in a low price elasticity of bundles with bulky articles simply because it is more difficult to adjust the size of a bundle of large-sized sweet potatoes than of small tomatoes.

Village women conduct their trade not only in market places but also in small stores where they disaggregate larger packages into the smaller units demanded by their customers. Rather than sell packets of ten cigarettes, which they buy from urban suppliers, they open these packets and sell single cigarettes. In so doing they make a small profit. Such small trade stores are important intermediaries between larger urban suppliers and the small-scale demand of rural consumers.

Cooked food preparations constitute another important income-generating activity for many rural women. The case study of Ibu Sai, a female petty entrepreneur in Java, indicates how such food sellers conduct their business. She prepares *gado-gado* (vegetables covered by a spicy peanut sauce) and *teripang* (a rice-based dish) and hawks it round an area which she has carved out for herself with the agreement of other local sellers of cooked food, all of whom together work like an oligopoly. Ibu Sai finds the sale of *gado-gado* a rewarding proposition. She uses her income to meet her family's subsistence needs since her husband earns insufficient money to provide for them. Besides the benefits her husband and children obviously derive from her earnings, they also have ready access to the food she prepares for sale. They thus do not need to spend money on buying these relishes and are therefore pleased with her success (Bangun 1985: 124). Many other villagers also appreciate the ready availability of cooked food, which adds variety to their diet.

Rural women not only cook, but in many areas also smoke certain items of food. For instance, in Ghana fish smoking is a major activity of coastal rural women. 'It is thought to employ as many as 40,000 women, who take the fish from their husbands, process and then market it' (Carr 1984: 16).

Food processing is another activity pursued by female entrepreneurs. In India *papad* rolling (preparing the dough for the *papal* crackers) is becoming an important source of income for increasing numbers of rural women. The seven women who started the Lijjat Pappad in 1959 repaid their initial debt of Rs80 with interest within six months. Right from the beginning Lijjat adopted strictly commercial marketing techniques:

> It appointed agents on a commission basis. . . . The Lijjat model shows how women can work at home on a put-out basis without the exploitation element so common elsewhere in India. It also shows how this non-exploitative approach does not necessarily mean a non-commercial one. Every attempt is made to maximize profits through normal commercial means but all workers are members and all share in the profits.
>
> (Carr 1984: 30)

Handicrafts, such as sewing, basket-making, and embroidery, which are normally thought of as being female activities, represent another entrepreneurial avenue by which rural women earn money. However, unstable markets for these goods cause difficulties. The experience of an Asian women's weaver co-operative when it tried to cater for a short-lived fashion demand in the United States illustrates the problems encountered in this context. The co-operative concentrated on the production of bleeding Madras, a checked cotton lunghi material with running colours, which temporarily appealed to Americans, and ignored the traditional market for sarongs used by the local men. 'Suddenly, the demand for bleeding Madras in the US ceased and the co-operatives found themselves with huge stocks and no market. This drove a number of co-operatives into bankruptcy and a large number of weavers to the point of starvation' (Dhamija 1981: 10).

The precarious nature of handicraft markets encourages increasing numbers of rural women to provide goods and services which are needed on a regular basis by most local communities, and which increasingly have to be paid for with cash. 'Many of the products, which are currently imported into villages from urban based factories or overseas, could be made in the neighbourhood if the appropriate technology, training and other support services were available' (Carr 1984: 9).

Production of basic consumer articles is gaining in importance among female entrepreneurs. Bothakga Handknits, started along those lines in 1974 by a woman in Botswana, provides a good example of this trend. The proprietor is a remarkably enterprising woman who is constantly on the look-out for new areas into which to expand. When she realized that many Botswanan schools were importing their uniforms and knitwear, which were items produced by her firm, she began trying to capture the market by approaching the head teachers of these schools with samples of uniforms and knitwear made by her firm. The response was overwhelming, 'with promises of future support coming in from those schools that had already placed orders with other suppliers' (Carr 1984: 60).

A bus service in Kenya represents another example, indicating how female entrepreneurs come to meet local needs. A group of Taita women in Mraru, realizing an urgent transport need, decided to buy a bus:

> It was agreed that each member, over time, should contribute at least K.Sh 200, which would be the value of the share. After 18 months, the group had saved 27,000 shillings and the group leader travelled to Mombassa to place an order for a bus with the Cooper Motor Corporation. Here it was found that a 21 seater bus would cost K.Shill 780 and that a down payment of K.Sh 47,800 would be needed before a bus could be released. The process of securing the extra money for the down payment by persuading a credit bank in Nairobi to give a loan to cover the rest of the purchase price was tortuous but successful and, five years after the idea had arisen, the bus arrived in Mraru. . . . The bus proved an excellent investment. In a year and a half, the debts were paid off and the group began a new savings account.
>
> (Carr 1984: 114)

They declared part of this as a dividend and the rest they targeted for the establishment of a retail shop in Mraru. As rural incomes increase, a greater proportion of income is spent on services as opposed to food and manufactured goods. Since women have traditionally offered a wide variety of services they are now strategically placed to capture at least a part of this growth sector. However, at the same time the increase in rural mechanization usually replaces women by men. 'Owner and operators of rural rice mills tend to be men as do pump mechanics and truck drivers, even though milling, water-drawing, lifting and transportation are traditionally female service activities' (Carr 1984: 108).

This brief summary of the different entrepreneurial activities pursued by rural women indicates not only the large and continuously growing number of female entrepreneurs, but also the changing pattern of their entrepreneurship in response to changing socio-economic conditions. However, almost all female enterprises still fall into the category of petty ventures.

WHY DO RURAL WOMEN BECOME MAINLY PETTY ENTREPRENEURS?

A number of constraints confine rural women to petty entrepreneurship. First, female-headed households put a heavy responsibility on women:

> It is estimated that, around the world today, one household out of every three is headed, *de facto*, by a woman. They might number 46 per cent of all households in Botswana, 40 per cent in Panama, 30 per cent in some rural areas in Kenya, 50 per cent in some areas in Latin America, 16 per cent in Cuba, and 20 per cent in the United States. Their plight tends, however, to be ignored by policy makers and development experts, since the increase in woman-headed households is obscured at the macro-data level, which is typically the only kind of data upon which development planning is based.... Very few countries include in their national census specific data on household heads by sex and even fewer cross-tabulate them by marital status, age, and economic activity.
>
> (Mandl 1980: 37)

Because of this lack of attention in development planning, much of the potential for female entrepreneurship has remained constrained and/or unrealized.

Second, low incomes and a shortage of funds, which are integral features of the lives of the majority of rural women, put further obstacles in the path of their entrepreneurship. Data for all countries indicate that while as many as 87 per cent of female heads of households earn less than about £500 per year, only 46 per cent of male heads do so (Mandl 1980: 37). The income differential between men and women is smaller in self-employment than in formal employment. In the Philippines, for instance, among employed workers females earn about 44 per cent less than males, while among self-employed workers, females earn only 31 per cent less. Women are thus understandably attracted to self-employment, but in general their low incomes and shortage of funds make it almost impossible for them to venture into larger businesses. Although women make up half the world's population they control only 1 per cent of its capital. Even when economic conditions improve, women's incomes and their working conditions do not seem to improve commensurately. Liberia is a typical case. Despite their control over and the importance of their roles in the food distribution systems, women seem to experience a deterioration in their marketing conditions relative to the general development of the economy.

Cultural norms also often adversely affect female entrepreneurship. In many societies expectations still prevail according to which women should operate solely in the domestic sphere. Many cultures still dictate that woman's primary role is in the home. Even 'if she takes on a job, she is expected to take care of her domestic responsibilities' (Iglesias 1984: 28). Illo, who studied the Bicol River Basin society in the Philippines, revealed that women, as well as men, agree that the woman's proper place is in the home (1977). If such cultural norms predominate, then women's entrepreneurial activities are confined to the home, where they do not conflict with their primary duties to watch their children and keep the household going.

In many traditional societies women's behaviour symbolizes the honour not only of their immediate family but often of their whole kin group. The concept of honour tends to carry special weight in all Muslim societies, particularly tribal ones such as the Pukhtun of Pakistan, among whom 'the direct laudatory equivalent to *Pakhto* is *saritob*, "manhood" or "honour"' (Ahmed and Ahmed 1981: 31). *Purdah*, the Muslim custom of female seclusion – which aims to protect women's purity – institutionalizes the restriction on women's spatial mobility. Yet even women in *purdah* have been reported as undertaking entrepreneurial roles. Many West African Muslim women are active traders, using their children as messengers (Hill 1962: 7) and there are women in Rajasthan in India, who within their *purdah* restrictions manage to conduct successful money-lending businesses (Cottam 1991: 37); in Pakistan many rural women take decisions regarding their households' economic activities because their menfolk are away working as migrant labourers in the oil states of the Middle East (Naveed-i-Rahat 1990: 52).

Female petty entrepreneurs 23

These are a few examples of the many that can be cited to show how female entrepreneurs assert themselves even under the most difficult conditions. Yet obviously the many problems facing them may limit the scale of their entrepreneurship.

WHAT PREVENTS WOMEN FROM BRANCHING OUT INTO LARGER ENTERPRISES?

The data presented so far clearly indicate the considerable entrepreneurial talent which exists among rural women. Why only so few female entrepreneurs manage to enlarge the scale of their operations may be explained by a number of factors.

Familial responsibilities and family ties, which are generally considered by men and women alike to be a woman's first duty, require women not only to bear many children but also to rear their offspring. Women's particularly disadvantaged position in entrepreneurial ventures reflects their multiple responsibilities (i.e. the care of children and the household, farming, etc.; see also Jones, Richardson and Hartshorn this volume). To release some of their time from familial responsibilities women have to rely for support on the members of their extended family. The stronger a rural woman is embedded in a wider kin network the less time she has to spend on her domestic duties, which enables her to spend more time on directly productive activities. On the other hand 'the extended family and the strong tradition of cooperation and reciprocity place enormous pressure on anyone with cash in hand to aid a needy kinsman or co-ethnic' (Lewis 1976: 140). Extended family ties are thus not altogether an untarnished blessing for female entrepreneurs.

Shortage of capital and lack of appropriate and unsecured credit represents one of the major obstacles to the expansion of female enterprises. Women lack the three most common forms of collateral required for credit: land title, cattle, or co-operative membership. 'In an area of one country where 30 per cent of household heads are females, only 7 per cent of those receiving credit are women' (Food and Agriculture Organization undated: 5).

Low levels of education and of technological know how are further important factors affecting female entrepreneurship:

> Out of the estimated 700 million people in the world who are illiterate, two-thirds are female.... Lack of time, fatigue, husband's disapproval, child care and domestic chores, and lack of

transportation severely limit women's opportunities to participate in non-formal and life-long education programmes.

(Mandl 1980: 30)

The gender-specific division of labour which still prevails in most societies means that female entrepreneurs are restricted to activities in which they have traditionally operated, such as food production, nutrition, health and child care. Significantly, little technological development has taken place in these tasks. In general women lack access to technical skill training as well as marketing or business training, which also obviously limits the range of their activities.

A too-narrow market horizon means that in many societies women are unlikely to diversify their entrepreneurial activities simply because they are unaware of the pattern of demand that prevails in the wider society. Their narrow market horizon is a function of their low educational level as well as of their multiple responsibilities which restrain their spatial mobility.

WHAT NEEDS TO BE DONE TO ENABLE MORE RURAL WOMEN TO REALIZE THEIR ENTREPRENEURAL POTENTIAL?

Positive action by international, national, and non-governmental agencies as well as by the private sector is a pre-condition for rural women to realize their entrepreneurial potential. The measures suggested below represent but a few of the many policy changes that are necessary in this context.

Some reduction of women's existing work commitments is essential before more women can be expected to take on additional responsibilities. 'As a rule, women work longer hours than men. Many carry multiple work loads in their households, labour force, and reproductive roles. Rural women often average an 18 hour day (Sivard 1985: 11). A reduction in the existing work load women have to carry can be brought about best by the introduction of appropriate domestic technologies, such as piped water supplies and solar energy stoves, accompanied by the establishment of rural creches.

Access to suitably administered credit, which means unsecured credit without many procedural requirements, is essential to help rural women overcome their shortage of capital. The *Production Credit for Rural Women in Nepal* (Joss 1988) and the *Small Business Credit for Samburu Women's Groups in Kenya* (Saidi 1988) represent such favourable credit facilities on a small scale. The Women's World Bank (WWB) aims to provide such credit on a global basis.

WWB is unique in its approach toward promoting women's economic development. Financing programmes are being created and implemented at local level using WWB's primary development tool – a loan guarantee contract. Guarantees to lending institutions offset the risk assumed by the lender, and enhance the availability of small operating and capital loans to women entrepreneurs. The WWB network of local affiliates has provided almost 25,000 loans to date . . . without a single reported default.

(Women's World Bank 1987)

Examples taken from the reports of the Women's World Bank illustrate the beneficial effect of suitable credit arrangements on female entrepreneurship. A dairy business run by an Indian woman increased the production and sale of buffalo milk through a WWB loan guarantee programme. As a mother of two, she knows how vital her milk production business is – the purchase of an additional buffalo means that more children have fresh milk; the woman's self-confidence and business acumen have soared.

A woman in Colombia started a bicycle repair shop in her home. Her business grew to include bicycle manufacturing, sales and rentals. Through WWB, a loan and management training course will allow her to double her business volume, give jobs to local residents, and to contribute to the development of her entire community (see also Jones this volume).

For Judy's Fruits, a client of Kenya Women Finance Trust Ltd and WWB, a loan meant the ability to buy equipment to produce the fresh fruit juice she sells to hotels in Nairobi, Kenya. Judy Nguiyi is thrilled that she no longer has to begin her day at 2 a.m., hand-squeezing 100 pounds of oranges.

Josephina Bastardo, an accessories manufacturer in the Dominican Republic, opened her business in 1985 with assets of about US 1 dollar; she earned three dollars on opening day. With the help of a US $1,000 loan from Banco del Comercio, guaranteed by the WWB affiliate, business expanded dramatically. Ms Bastardo now has 14 employees and revenues equivalent of US $120,000 a year.

These cases clearly show the important contribution that appropriately administered credit makes to the expansion of female enterprises.

The provision of appropriate training facilities constitutes another vital element in the promotion of female entrepreneurship. Women need to acquire not only a variety of technical skills to enable them to venture into more remunerative businesses, but they also require basic training in accountancy and business management. Many of the existing illiterate female petty entrepreneurs have little precise knowledge about what level of returns, where and in which period in the year the various activities they want to pursue will yield. Simplified accountancy and business management training using appropriate visual aids is thus urgently needed to help improve these women's business acumen.

Professionally conducted location-specific resource and market surveys are another essential prerequisite for potential female entrepreneurs. These would enable them to match demand with available supplies. Rural women, with their narrow market horizon, have difficulty in establishing what goods or services for which there is a reasonably steady demand to offer. In some parts of the Third World, where mulberry trees grow, local women cannot exploit their potential for sericulture because they do not know how to rear silk worms nor are they aware of the large demand for silk. In Serowe (Botswana), for instance, there is an abundance of mulberry trees yet local women are not aware of how sericulture is conducted. To start a silk industry in Botswana, a country totally dependent on imports of cotton and artificial fibre cloth, seems an attractive proposition, but only to those who know the process of sericulture and can estimate the demand for silk (Epstein 1979: 22). Local women have been oblivious of this potential income-earning opportunity. This case throws into relief the fundamental importance of locally specific resource and market surveys in the expansion of female entrepreneurship. Once this information is available to rural women we can be confident that increasing numbers of them will branch out into new and more profitable business ventures.

This chapter has tried to show some of the entrepreneurial activities in which women are engaged, and their ingenuity in succeeding as petty entrepreneurs. It has also outlined the difficulties female entrepreneurs face, some of which also apply to rural men, and what needs to be done to encourage more rural women to take up business activity and to operate on a larger scale. To enable more rural women to realize their entrepreneurial potential and to succeed in larger ventures poses a challenge to developers which unless met will be detrimental not only to the quality of rural life, but more important it will also adversely affect the overall development process.

NOTE

1 This chapter appears by kind permission of I.T. Publications where it was first published in Shailendra Vaye Karnam (ed.) (1990) *When the Harvest is In*.

3 Rural women

Mary Jones

INTRODUCTION

Today, living in a comfortable modernized cottage within a few miles of the Welsh border, in one of the most beautiful areas of England, it would be easy to romanticize about the life of rural women in the West; to overlook the loneliness and depression; to forget the sheer physical hardship of living without electricity or a piped water supply. However, I well remember, less than thirty years ago, pumping water, carrying buckets, doing everything by hand. The isolated farm cottage had no running water, no electricity, and open fires which constantly needed replenishing. Life in the country can be very hard. Sara Delamont (1980: 132) identified seven themes of rural life, the first being 'the unremitting domestic toil' and the second 'the importance of agricultural work' which meant rural women often had to shoulder an additional burden outside the home. Furthermore, many farmers' wives were expected to make a significant contribution to the household budget by selling eggs and poultry.

The Industrial Revolution, with its new opportunities, inevitably changed the lives of rural men and women. Exodus from the countryside gained momentum as wage earners and their families moved to the towns and cities in search of a better lifestyle. The rural population was 'pulled' into new jobs by the prospect of regular work and regular wages in the new industries, although living and working conditions were often appalling. At the same time, agricultural employment declined as mechanization on the farms increased. Lack of alternative opportunities, remoteness, and few, if any, amenities contributed to the depopulation of the rural areas.

The elderly lost their family and neighbours, and houses were left empty. Some became derelict, others were bought by wealthy outsiders as second homes. The situation was poignantly described by the Welsh Language Society in the early 1970s, 'Some of these elderly will die from sheer loneliness – and more properties will become vacant. The village becomes a half-deserted collection of buildings. Its community spirit is gone' (quoted in Mahon 1973: 12). Services gradually decline – local traders leave, the local school is forced to close, the bus service is reduced – which forces more people to leave. 'There are fewer people in the village. The second home owners have killed a community and replaced it with empty houses' (quoted in Mahon 1973: 12).

The economic and social effects of allowing such a situation to persist are clear, although the case against the second home owner is unproven. Other factors must be considered. Professor J. K. Galbraith saw migration as the efficient course:

> If a locality is declining – if power, transportation, raw-material supplies, consumer taste, or the tax laws have given other areas or countries an advantage – then one should encourage the people to leave. Mobility means efficiency. It is true that the ties of family, friends, pastor and priest, countryside and mere inertia may make this a Draconian and even cruel prescription. But it is the efficient course.
>
> (Galbraith 1962: 232)

RURAL AREAS

Fortunately the government has pursued a more humane, if less efficient, policy than that advocated by Galbraith. Since 1909, government support has been directed to the rural areas, first through the Rural Industries Bureau under the umbrella of the Development Commission and, from 1968, through the Council for Small Industries in Rural Areas and the Development Commission. In April 1988, these two bodies were merged to form the Rural Development Commission, which has the responsibility for keeping under review 'all matters relating to the economic and social development of rural areas in England' (Rural Development Commission 1988). The policy seems to have been effective. The flow of people from the rural areas to the industrial areas has been reversed. From 1971 to 1988, population in the 'remoter largely rural areas' of England and Wales increased from 9.48 per cent of the total population in 1971 to 10.85 per cent by 1988 (Office of Population Censuses and Surveys 1990). This has been at the expense of Greater London, the Metropolitan Districts and the cities. Government assistance combined with social, cultural, demographic, economic and other changes means that rural depopulation has ceased to be a problem.

However, many of these rural areas have a marked age imbalance in the structure of the population caused by the continuing out-migration of young people and young families in search of work and the in-migration of older, often retired couples. Unless more support is given to provide jobs and low cost housing for young people and young families, rural areas may become merely a haven for the retired. Alternatively, because of their remoteness and natural beauty many may become simply a playground for the holidaymaker. For the local population, neither of these developments will secure the socially and economically balanced, viable communities which are necessary to support a full range of facilities for themselves and their children. Families who remain in the rural areas face increasing problems as agricultural incomes and employment decline, education, health, and other services are centralized, and housing and transport costs rise. Women who want to work have few opportunities, wages are low, and travel without a second car often impossible (see also Epstein this volume).

One way of supplementing the family income has always been through petty or small scale entrepreneurship. Many rural women engage in dressmaking, baking, craft, and other activities for family and friends. An increasing number are putting their businesses on a more formal footing in response to the demand from tourists, in-migrants, and other women. Labour Force Survey figures from 1984 to 1987 show a rising trend in the number of married and non-married women turning to full-time and part-time self-employment (Department of Employment 1988a). The enterprise culture of the 1980s has given entrepreneurship a new emphasis.

SHROPSHIRE

In Shropshire, the most substantial growth has been outside the rural areas. The new town of Telford has developed numerous enterprises and consequent new job opportunities. Figures for those in employment have grown from 36,191 in 1971 to 42,279 in 1980, and to 58,182 in 1989. Most of the jobs have been created by small and medium sized companies; there are relatively few large employers. Over half of the firms in the manufacturing sector and three-quarters in the service sector employ less than ten people (Telford Development Corporation 1990).

Telford received substantial investment, both from the State and from private enterprise, which has attracted new entrepreneurs and helped to ensure its future. In contrast, South Shropshire has received little investment. Its small towns and villages remain comparatively quiet and unspoilt. Until the nineteenth century higglers (see Epstein this volume) traded in the small street markets of country towns like Ludlow and Bishop's Castle. The ancestors of the J. P. Wood family were higglers trading in chickens, turkeys, ducks, eggs, and rabbits, although by the end of the nineteenth century they described themselves more formally as 'poultry dealers'. Jane Overton, who married John Percy Wood in 1913, had established her shop at London House, Market Street, Craven Arms in the early 1900s (Midland Poultry Holdings 1984). From this base J. P. Wood & Sons developed until in 1964 it was floated on the Stock Exchange as Midland Poultry Holdings.

The potential for development is clear: the area has a strong enterprise culture. The high propensity to self-employment among both men and women is evident from employment statistics. In South Shropshire twice as many men and women are self-employed compared to the West Midlands area as a whole.

SOUTH SHROPSHIRE

Yet South Shropshire remains one of the most sparsely populated regions of England, although it is less than one hour's drive from Telford and from the West Midland conurbation. Most of the district is designated an Area of Outstanding Natural Beauty. These factors contribute to the area's character, to its quality of life and to its problems. South Shropshire, in common with other remoter rural areas, suffers from a marked age imbalance in its population, a lack of diversity of opportunities, low wages and insufficient low cost housing for local families. However, small factory units have been built in half a dozen locations. Further support has been given for the regeneration of the auction market and for the transformation of the comprehensive school into a thriving community college in Bishop's Castle. The Rural Development Commission has played an important part in the area's economy since the first scheme for assistance was approved in 1974. In 1989 South Shropshire was designated one of three pilot areas for a Rural Initiative under the auspices of Business in the Community, thus ensuring further support for local enterprise.

Amid this burgeoning activity, a significant fact emerges: women play an important role in the economy of the area. In the early 1980s, female self-employment as a percentage of all female employment was

32 *Women in business*

11.7 per cent in South Shropshire, compared to 6.4 per cent in the county of Shropshire (Shropshire County Council 1983), and 5.2 per cent in the West Midlands (Creigh et al. 1986). One can speculate that many factors contribute to this high percentage of women entrepreneurs. Some women might prefer to be self-employed. Other women, because of their partner's employment, school hours or parental obligations might find it difficult to take paid employment outside the home. In a rural area these difficulties are compounded by the lack of job opportunities, low wages, and the scarcity and cost of transport. Family, school, and other factors might have an influence on whether a woman chose employment or self-employment. More information was needed on the women entrepreneurs, their background, constraints and motivation. Previous studies of women entrepreneurs have tended to focus on urban areas or on fairly wide geographical areas. A study in a rural area with a strong enterprise culture would, it was felt, provide a new perspective and offer an interesting contribution to the debate.

THE SOUTH SHROPSHIRE STUDY

Early in 1989 I selected twelve women to give an indication of the wide range of entrepreneurs and enterprises in South Shropshire. The age range of the sample range was from 24 to 82. A semi-structured interview technique was used to obtain both quantitative and qualitative data. Initially, a detailed questionnaire to obtain quantitative data from a larger sample was considered. However, this method was rejected as it was felt that the qualitative data would be more valuable for the purpose of this research (see Carter this volume).

The research had five aims. These were to obtain data on personal circumstances, schooling, employment and businesses; to explore in more detail aspects of family life and business experience; to identify areas of commonality between respondents and findings from other research; to identify and examine the multiple roles of women entrepreneurs; to ascertain whether or not women feel they can help one another and ways in which they felt they could be helped.

The significant factors identified in this study of women entrepreneurs were the family background of the daughters; the impact of socialization in the family of origin and at school; education, training, and employment; and the effect of marriage and motherhood, including the attitude of husband and children. The crucial points seem to be the support which the woman received from either the family of origin or the family of procreation, and the training which she had undertaken.

Family of origin

In terms of self-employment a number of writers have identified a family relationship. Goldthorpe and his colleagues identified a 'tradition of self-employment' amongst male respondents in the early 1970s (Goldthorpe 1980: 258). Studies of female entrepreneurs, have found a connection with self-employment through fathers (Watkins and Watkins 1984; Carter and Cannon 1988a). Watkins and Watkins also identified mother's self-employment as a factor in their research. In South Shropshire nine of the twelve women entrepreneurs had family connections with self-employment; four, including the only two local women, were farmers' daughters, one father had owned a chemist's shop, another a tyre factory, two were managers who had become self-employed, and one's adopted father was a self-employed builder. Only three of the women entrepreneurs had no family connection with self-employment: they were daughters of an accountant, a civil engineer and the adopted daughter of a minister. A grandfather's garage provided further evidence of entrepreneurial family connections, and all four children had become self-employed. In the late 1980s it seems that Goldthorpe's 'tradition of self-employment' may apply equally to the daughters of the 'petty bourgeoisie'. Thus family and family background appeared important in terms of orientation to self-employment. This concurs with Curran's comments on the importance of 'the transmission of the culture and knowledge of small-scale economic activity' (Curran 1986: 47).

Some of the choices and constraints which women feel about work may be formed at an early age. Daughters' perception of what they can do or achieve relates to what they see parents doing and to what they themselves have been allowed or encouraged to do in their family of origin. The daughters all seemed to have been brought up either in a family which expected that the daughters would earn their own living or in a working environment, where they helped on the farm looking after the animals, or in the shop, in the garden or with the younger children in the family. One farmer's daughter described life on the farm in terms of 'whatever needed doing, everyone helped'. Another, an only daughter, helped more outside on the farm than inside the home and worked with her father on Saturdays selling farm produce from a market stall. A third recalled her childhood as 'you were brought up that it was no disgrace to scrub the floor, clean the shed, milk the goat'. Thus the majority were used to working hard when they were girls and were, therefore, well prepared for self-employment.

Girls must be influenced not only by factors in their own lives but by factors which affect other women, particularly their close relatives. Allen (1982) identified the lack of knowledge about the female members of the family, their relationship with each other and with the male members of the family, as a serious problem. Therefore in our research mother's and grandmother's work and occupation were examined as well as that of the respondent's father. In their early lives, seven of the entrepreneurs had seen their mothers taking on roles in addition to those of wife and mother, either as employees or as workers in a family business. One, after working as a nurse, had taken a degree in sociology, another was a headmistress. Mothers who themselves worked, either on the farm, in the family business or outside, may have provided significant role models for their daughters. In two of the families there was evidence of a tradition of working women (Burr 1986: 13). Three grandmothers, two in the one family, also lived with the household at the time their granddaughters were growing up. It would be valuable to know more about these and other relationships and the effect they have on a daughter's and granddaughter's aspirations and achievements.

A further significant factor affecting girls was the size of the family and their position in it. Other studies of business owners, female managers and professional women have found a high incidence of only, or oldest children, but particularly girls without male siblings. Hertz suggests that: 'In practice the absence of sons meant that at the basic level of everyday family life, where the first differentiation between male and female offspring took place, the daughters were not discriminated against' (Hertz 1986: 86). She felt that this gave the daughters an advantage in later life, particularly in the world of business. The South Shropshire women seemed to follow this pattern: five were, or had been brought up, as only or oldest girls from all-daughter families, and one was the youngest of four daughters. In total seven were, or had been brought up as, the oldest girl. Three girls had older brothers, one was the middle child, two had younger brothers. In two of the three families, where the daughter was the youngest, the brothers went away to boarding schools at eleven and in the third family the daughter herself went away to school, effectively reducing the differentiation between siblings. The middle daughter described doing everything with the two older boys on the family farm. Of the two oldest girls, one took responsibility for her two younger brothers while her mother worked and was encouraged in her pursuit of outdoor activities; the other described helping her father in the garden and felt she became the 'boss' of the family because of her grammar school education. Thus there is evidence that the majority of daughters had not been socialized in the family of origin to a subordinate gender role.

The numbers are too small to say whether there is a tendency amongst self-employed women towards non-traditional female areas. However, a number of the respondents commented on the fact that they were 'one of the boys', a 'toughy', or had 'like interests with the boys'. One girl had played football with the men on Saturday afternoons. There seemed to be evidence of the girls receiving or searching for equal treatment with their brothers and/or the boys of their acquaintance. This reinforces the view that as they grew up these girls were not socialized to a particular feminine role.

School

Socialization and experience in school may widen girls' perceptions or merely reinforce traditional gender roles. Five of the girls had been to single sex schools, one of whom transferred to a co-educational secondary modern school at thirteen. One other girl had been to a secondary modern school, two to a comprehensive, and four to selective grammar schools, one of which was private. Four others had been to private schools, one as a weekly boarder, two as full boarders; one of the boarding schools was co-educational.

The respondents' experience of school varied from positive, 'smashing', to completely negative. One said, 'didn't like school, no discipline'. Another had 'no respect for teachers', or the 'ridiculous rules'. A third was classified as a 'difficult pupil' and 'didn't like authority'. Of these two had been to secondary modern and one to a comprehensive school. Experience in the private schools ranged from comments exemplifying the feeling that school taught the person 'to stand on your own two feet', discipline, self-discipline and getting on with people, to dislike of being a weekly boarder in a small local boarding school. Both of the girls from mixed grammar schools were highly critical of their treatment in 'A' level mathematics. One was told, 'I'm not having a woman in my maths class', but overcame this objection and the other was ignored as the only girl in the group. Two of the younger respondents had been able to choose woodwork in preference to cookery or needlework. Interestingly, however, it was two of the older respondents who reported equality at school in terms of boys knitting, and girls and boys playing hockey and tennis together.

Educational qualifications, training and employment

The women interviewed had a wide range of educational qualifications. Two had obtained degrees, whereas three had left school without any qualifications. Others had gained A level and/or O level (or their previous equivalents) or the Certificate of Secondary Education qualification. From this small study choice of self-employment does not seem to depend on the type of school, the girls' experience of school or the level of qualifications obtained at school.

Although school qualifications did not seem a crucial factor, further and higher education and training were important. Nine of the women had undertaken post-sixteen college courses at some time in their lives, including the two with degrees. Of the three who had not undertaken any post-school training, one had worked her way up to the position of manageress, an indication of significant on-the-job training. Only two women were running their businesses without any formal training, and one of these subsequently ceased trading. This suggests that women without the prerequisite skills may need to consider undertaking training or obtaining qualifications before starting in business. A lack of training places a severe constraint on women who enter self-employment (see Epstein in this volume).

Five of the women were using, in their own businesses, experience which they had gained as employees, but for others previous employment was less significant. Only one woman had started her business from skills acquired whilst at home. She had bought a second-hand knitting machine at an auction and taken orders at home before opening her retail outlet. She had also taken an A level in needlework at the age of forty with young students at the local sixth form college. This reinforces the importance of training in the context of self-employment.

Self-employment

The 'pull' to self-employment for this sample was strong, perhaps because of family background. Two of the women had gone straight into self-employment from college while another had retrained as a hairdresser in her twenties and started her business immediately after training. Three had decided at a comparatively young age that they would prefer to be their own boss. These five women, all without children, seemed to have chosen self-employment as a career. Two had never been employees and three were farmers' daughters. Among all of them there was a clear motivation to be their own boss. This contrasts with the position of many Third World women who are 'pushed' into self-employment through the lack of alternative means of generating an income (see Epstein in this volume).

Family support

In starting their businesses both of the single women had parental support. The youngest of the sample welcomed her father's business advice (he had run his own company), and his practical help. He was in fact working in the shop on the afternoon of the interview. One of the older respondents had received a loan of one hundred pounds in 1947 from her father which she had paid back within two years. Being a daughter in a family where there was both practical support and encouragement, which came particularly from fathers, was thus beneficial for them.

The three other women without children had all been in business prior to marriage/domestic partnership. In two cases parental support had not only been important in starting a business but had also continued after marriage/partnership. One mother helped to decorate the hairdressing salon and continues to 'lend a hand' when she is not too busy on the farm. In the other case both parents deliver publicity leaflets for their daughter's business. Being a daughter with parental support can be a bonus in business terms but as in the second case, where the daughter is becoming increasingly concerned about her mother's health, also brings an added burden in terms of responsibility as parents grow older.

Although these three women business owners claimed to accord priority to their husband/partner, their businesses were clearly an important part of their lives. One domestic partner had no interest in the woman's business, which she described as 'my business'. Both wives were aware that their husbands 'felt' they were working too hard. One of the women entrepreneurs had taken on an employee to ease the situation. The other worked three nights a week in a local residential home to help finance her enterprise which engaged her for seven days each week. Two of the husbands helped out with domestic matters but the third partner would have to make considerable adjustment if he was to take on more responsibility in this sphere. Women with their own businesses face a difficult task in prioritising between their dual roles of wife and business owner. Women with children face the task of balancing three roles successfully.

All those women who had become self-employed after marriage had children at the time they started in business. The incentive to succeed seemed to stem in a number of cases from adverse life experiences: divorce, an invalid husband, or the early loss of one or both parents. When the whole family depend on the business, either because of illness of one partner or because both husband and wife work together, there seems to be a strong incentive to succeed.

Husbands had played a significant part in the formation of three of the businesses. In two cases husband and wife were directors and one of the couples worked together, while in the third the husband retained his interest in the company. The first two of these companies were by far the largest employers. The third husband seemed to have lost his initial enthusiasm. In the other businesses the husbands' involvement was limited to discussing problems with the entrepreneurial wife. Overall the existence of husbands and children appeared to encourage the women in their business activity and to enhance motivation to succeed.

Multiple Roles

The attitudes and expectations of the women differed, as did their priorities. Three were prepared to prioritize their role of mother where two found this more difficult. The director of the largest firm, who had four children and worked with her husband, said, 'you just juggle'. Her sister-in-law commented, 'I don't know how she did it', but there was no need to 'farm the children out' because the business was run from home until 1979, by which time the children were grown up. The second, a younger director with three school-age children and expecting another baby, was in the fortunate position of running her residential home from a site adjacent to the family home. As a business owner, wife and mother she was coping with many demands simultaneously. She worked long hours, including being on duty in the home four nights per week. These two women, with their husbands' support, appeared to have adjusted to the multiple roles of business owner, wife and mother, although in one family the children were grown up.

Two others, both with retail outlets, seemed more constrained by the conventional role of wife and mother. They were unable to devote as much time as they would like to the business and were frustrated by the conflict of roles. One felt she was 'squashing' herself. She was the only other mother interviewed with a school age child and had no doubts about the role of mother. 'You choose to have children. You look after them until they're five', which is what she had done. This mother, wife and business owner described doing 'everything in the house for ten years'. She found housework frustrating, in spite of having a small studio at home. However, since she opened a retail outlet/workshop eighteen months ago, she has 'put her foot down' and gained a degree of symmetry in the domestic situation (Young and Willmott 1973). She usually stays at home with her daughter on Saturday and stops making jewellery when her daughter comes to the shop from school because she finds it difficult to concentrate. If her daughter, aged 9, was ill she would stay at home. The second one had teenage children (17 and 19 years) but would still close her shop if necessary to cope with a domestic crisis. At first she had thought she could remain open during lunch hours but because her husband prefers to lunch at home and not at the back of the shop she felt unable to remain open. Interviewing her illustrated this very well. The interview was conducted in two parts because the first session had ended promptly at one o'clock when her husband arrived to give her a lift home. The particular problems these two women faced stemmed from running their businesses single-handed in premises away from their homes, and being constrained by husband and children.

The third retail outlet was owned by a woman with grown up children. The business was large enough to employ one full-time and several part-time members of staff. Again the children were a priority: 'you have to make them – all the roles – fit in'. She had done this by getting up very early to deal with domestic matters. She 'couldn't cope with being a wife and mother without the business'. Although she discussed business problems with her husband, she would not want to be in partnership with him or anyone else, and preferred 'business on my own'. This business owner did not seem to feel the same constraints as the other two and is now separated from her husband.

To the extent that wives had less time to spend on domestic matters, a restructuring of domestic roles seemed to have taken place in several cases. Some husbands were prepared to take on greater domestic responsibility, not always without conflict, while others preferred to buy more labour saving devices for the home. Modern technology eases some of the burden of domestic chores and may enable more women to devote time to their businesses or to other activities (see Epstein in this volume).

Two women who were no longer married did not face the conflict of being both a wife and a business owner. Both had started their businesses in response to adverse circumstances, in one case divorce and in the other the husband's illness, in order to provide a living for the family. For one, her role as mother had influenced her decision to become a farmer and her son was employed on the farm. Divorced five years ago, she had faced personal loss and her husband's business failure. She described borrowing a considerable sum to help finance the farm, building up the flock of sheep from twenty-seven to 300, and improving the quality of the flock. She had for the first time in her life taken part-time work with one of the other business owners interviewed, to help the family finances. She sees her own daughter, aged 23, having a very different married life from that of herself or her own mother. With hindsight, she feels that the asymmetrical relationship not only denied her a role in her husband's business, but also denied her husband a part in the upbringing of their children. With her children's support, she has found a new kind of 'freedom', a smaller house, less money, but more responsibility for her own life.

The other, at 82, living in a modern bungalow, a widow for twenty years, and the oldest of the entrepreneurs in the survey, still takes paying guests, and offers morning coffee, afternoon teas and meals without any paid help. In addition, she undertakes voluntary work for the Multiple Sclerosis Society, of which she is a founder member, and she is also writing her autobiography. She described the many changes in her life, from thinking when she married at the age of 32 that the hard times were over (she had been an adopted child, and had worked from the age of 13), to finding out, after a few years of marriage, that her husband would, if he lived, be an invalid for the rest of his life; by this time her fifth child was on the way. 'I realized I was the breadwinner. I knew I had to pull my socks up.' With six children, an invalid husband, paying guests and the farm, the hours were long and the work hard. When asked about problems, she summed it up by saying, there was 'no time to be conscious of the problems'.

Problems

The other women gave examples of a variety of problems. Four of the women gave instances of difficulties with their banks, which one had resolved by changing to her father's bank. One woman who had received financial assistance, a grant and weekly allowance from the Craft Council, felt that women do not research enough about what help is available.

Several of the women were clear about their market segment and the concepts of marketing, others were experiencing difficulty in this field. Five, all in crafts and catering, admitted (or had been told) that they were undercharging (see Carter in this volume). Some of the women identified problems with customers. For example, the experience with engineering customers who were not accustomed to dealing with women were described by one woman in the following way: 'they are certainly not going to tell you – a woman – what they want' and 'wouldn't think you knew anything technical'. Others had problems with suppliers' representatives and insurance agents who automatically say, 'I'll see your husband'. Nevertheless, only two of the women expressed the feeling that it was harder for women in business. In their own ways, using their many skills, the majority had decided that being feminine and pleasant was to their advantage. One said, 'to support not gain'. 'Be natural' said the oldest respondent.

There seemed to be a low incidence or perception of gender related problems among the women interviewed (Carter and Cannon 1988a: 568). This may be a reflection of the socialization of the women both at home and at school or the degree of family support they had received. Or it may be due to the types of business, mainly dealing with women and employing women, or the location in a rural area. The difficulty of time and time management, of 'juggling' roles and responsibilities, seemed to outweigh all the other problems. None of the women had succeeded in combining a business that was not home-based with pre-school age children and one with a school age child was finding it difficult to manage child care and her business.

Of the businesses originally identified, one had ceased trading three months before the interview. The woman had been in partnership with her younger, unemployed sister, who had received support from the Enterprise Allowance Scheme. After six months the younger sister had lost interest and had left when the Enterprise Allowance ceased. The older sister continued on her own for twelve months, but financial problems and family pressure proved too much. She was the only woman interviewed with a pre-school age child, whom she took to work with her during the day. Without the family, more time could have been devoted to the business, but there was resentment that she was going 'down there' again, particularly in the evenings and at weekends. This woman was determined that she would go into business again, on her own, when the three children were older. She had thoroughly enjoyed the two years and felt she had learned a lot from the experience.

Networking and assistance

Few of the women met many other women in business, perhaps because of the rural location in which they worked. One reason given for not wanting to meet more women in business was lack of time, but one woman thought 'them' bossy and another said they were overbearing. When asked 'Do you think women in business can help one another?' the answers ranged from 'Yes' to 'No help'. Two would prefer men and women to help one another and two others felt that they did not get on well with other women. Given the small numbers of women respondents too much emphasis cannot be put on the negative responses. However, they do indicate an element of contradictoriness in gender relations and an adoption of stereotyping of women entrepreneurs by women entrepreneurs. There was a general criticism of the lack of incentives for some women entrepreneurs given the employment potential of some businesses they ran, but few of the women could identify help that might have been useful to them. One felt working in a retail business, prior to opening her own, would have given her valuable experience and another younger woman thought more role models of women in business would be useful.

These women had proved, or were proving to themselves and to others, that, mainly with family support, they could achieve satisfaction, independence and responsibility for the business, their employees and their own lives. Little significance was attached to financial rewards. The words of the women themselves summarized their feelings about women starting up their own businesses: 'don't let the snags put you off'; 'stand up for yourself'; 'you've got to be brave'; 'you don't think you can'. These show the women were aware of obstacles and discouragement that are common for women setting up their own business but were concerned to encourage others to overcome them.

EIGHTEEN MONTHS LATER

The women were interviewed again eighteen months later. One had ceased trading and another had decided that she needed to acquire new skills and was changing direction. Otherwise all the women were still running their businesses. The same interview technique was used as on the first occasion, but with particular attention being paid to the areas identified as important in the earlier interview; these were training and support. More emphasis was attached to future plans, including training, and to future policy (Jones 1990).

From the material gained in the second interview it emerged that the level of educational qualifications which the women had obtained in school was proving a significant factor in business development. The women with few, if any, qualifications from school had not undertaken any training since starting their businesses, nor did they plan to do so. One of these had ceased trading, and two of the other businesses showed evidence of decline as measured by the number of employees. Those without qualifications do not appear to value training and this may have an adverse effect on their businesses. Business growth and plans for future development and training were clearly concentrated in the half who had O levels or equivalent, or higher level, qualifications. Women with higher educational qualifications appear more likely to value training for business or employment and this probably increases the prospect of business development and growth. This suggests that positive efforts must be made by training agencies to identify and encourage women with less successful school careers to undertake training, otherwise poor achievement at school may hinder business development and increase the risk of business failure.

There were major changes in five of the women's personal lives. Two women had new babies, three had separated from their husband/domestic partner. The baby had placed an additional strain on the mother with three school age children. She seemed tired and was finding it difficult to manage her time between the multiple roles of wife, mother and business owner. The other woman with a new baby seemed unprepared for the effect motherhood would have on her business. She had thought 'it wouldn't make that much difference'. Although she was in the fortunate position of being able to work partly from home, she was unable to do as much 'workwise' because she felt it would be detrimental 'babywise'. Coping with pre-school age children clearly presents a problem for some women with their own businesses.

Separation from husbands or a domestic partner also seemed to have created problems. One woman had ceased trading and the two other businesses showed evidence of decline. These three women were those identified above as having few if any educational qualifications. It appears that education, training, business growth and marriage are all closely correlated. The women whose marital relationship had proved stable seemed to be more successful in business, and whilst it is not possible to identify cause and effect, this sample suggests that in a rural area family life and a good education are important.

However, when the women were asked if they saw themselves as successful a different pattern emerged. The three women who did not regard themselves as successful would by external criteria be judged to be so. One was a director of the largest firm and one a director of the second largest firm. They were all married, had higher educational qualifications and two were mothers with young babies. Their negative response centred on time management and the difficulties inherent in achieving a balance between their multiple roles.

Women who in their business and personal lives were on the face of it less successful, nevertheless defined themselves as successful in terms of the criteria of personal happiness and feelings of satisfaction. The Birmingham Women's Enterprise Development Agency has found that their clients often defined success in fairly simple terms. For example: 'picking up the 'phone to make an appointment with a business adviser' or 'completing a business plan'. This led then to the conclusion that 'In our view, a woman is successful if she has learned self-confidence and skills which have been useful in her making an educated choice about her life options, thus bringing her happiness and fulfilment.' (Birmingham Women's Enterprise Development Agency 1990). They also included 'organizing your time and family commitments in order to manage tasks' as a fairly simple definition of success, but as my research showed this is not simple and can create feelings of failure.

Attending a business course, evaluating a business plan or running a business may be a good way of achieving personal development. Since starting their own businesses the women entrepreneurs I interviewed felt that they had become more independent, assertive, and confident, particularly in their dealings with people and in approaching business matters. The importance of women's businesses would seem to lie in the personal growth of the women as much as in business growth, although perhaps personal growth is a prerequisite for business development.

CONCLUSION

Women entrepreneurs have an important and increasing contribution to make to the family budget and to the prosperity of the community, but it is clear that they may face many problems. This research identifies a number of serious issues and implications for women and for women entrepreneurs, particularly those in rural areas. Women who wish to work may choose between employment and self-employment depending on their individual circumstances, constraints, and motivations. These may stem from socialization in the family of origin and at school, from educational achievement and subsequent training, and from personal and domestic circumstances. Prospective women entrepreneurs must give serious consideration to some or all of the following questions. What type of business should I start? Will it involve weekend and/or evening work? Is this realistic, bearing in mind other commitments? Where is the business to be located (particularly if there are children to be considered)? Should I consider training and improving educational qualifications whilst the children are young, with a view to starting in business at a later date?

I found the self-confidence, the determination, and the positive attitude of these rural women entrepreneurs an inspiration. This brief account of their experiences may inspire other women to consider training, employment or self-employment. There is a need for policy and decision makers in education, training, and the enterprise agencies to become more sensitive to the needs of women, and more aware of the potential of women's businesses. It seems that success depends on longer term support, and more in-depth counselling, than is at present available through the support agencies. Rural women who, from choice or necessity, manage their own businesses deserve more support and greater recognition. They are making a valuable contribution to the rural economy.

4 The minerva matrix women entrepreneurs
Their perception of their management style

Nadine Vokins

This chapter is concerned with a study of successful women entrepreneurs in the city of Bristol. It gives the reasons for initiating the research, the nature of the project, and its main findings. It concludes with reflections from some of the women at a seminar held two years later, together with implications for management development in the future.

BACKGROUND

Working in a predominantly male organization, and meeting and working on various courses with other women managers similarly placed, inevitably led to the shared realization that our problems, frustrations, and need for new strategies were caused by the fundamental constraint of operating in male-constructed environments.

This was highlighted at two seminars of South West Women into Management (SWWIM) which focused particularly on this constraint. The first concluded that the problem for women managers is that the stereotypes of women and of managers are in conflict, so that in some situations it is inevitable that women managers

(a) lack credibility
(b) may lack a clear sense of identity – there are few role models
(c) will have more problems with communication and in being accepted than will their male counterparts.

The second seminar examined two issues. The first was that women prefer a democratic style of management whereas men prefer authoritarian styles. The second dealt with the implications following from this that perhaps women cannot respond contingently, responding to varying situations with differing management styles, but only from their beliefs about an ideal or preferred style of management. The conclusions were that despite many women's dislike of hierarchical relationships and their belief that a more co-operative structure and culture is possible, they recognize that it is not possible to be accepted as a manager unless one complies with the existing hierarchical system. Once women are accepted and perceived as successful managers they may then be able to modify the system to some extent. 'With more acceptance and power, women could achieve substantial changes' (Peggy Henning, Chairman). The strategies suggested by Judi Marshall (1984) concerning the enhancement of confidence, coping with prejudice, confrontation, and competition were examined. Those suggesting copying male behaviour patterns and capitalizing on stereotyped female characteristics were rejected in favour of using knowledge-based professionalism and clear, unambiguous communication styles emanating from a strong sense of identity. These remain crucial points in the debate about management styles.

Accepted management and leadership theories appear to be modelled on male behaviour, perceptions and values, as do most management courses. A review of management literature reveals that comparatively little analysis or research has been done regarding the style in which women manage when they begin with *tabula rasa*, that is when they do not inherit male structures or male expectations. There have been varied statements regarding women's values, strengths, and managerial styles. These usually relate to research in longstanding organizations. Little study has been carried out of the ways in which women choose to organize themselves, to relate to each other and to develop their business (Cuba et al. 1983). There has been an almost complete neglect of the contribution that women make to the formulation and growth of business, particularly small scale enterprise (Goffee and Scase 1985).

Judi Marshall (1984) makes the point that effort is directed at a one-way traffic of socializing women into the prevailing male world with few, if any, opportunities for women to exert reciprocal influence on that world. Equal opportunities as it is officially prescribed and offered is thus a sexist interpretation.

Some research has, however, been conducted into aspects of female management style, though still within the male-dominated constraint. Two researchers in the United States administered hard-style inventories to both male and female business managers (Boulgarides 1984; Burke 1979). They concluded that, according to Allport's System of Values, and French and Bell's Decision-style Inventory, there were no significant differences between male and female business values and decision-making styles.

Studies of female entrepreneurs by Leah Hertz in the United States and David and Jean Watkins in the UK, for example, have analysed factors like the educational background of the entrepreneurs, their position in the family, and the predominance among their parents of small business ownership (Clutterbuck and Devine 1987). The success of female entrepreneurs has also been investigated and compared with those of males. It is rare, however, to find analyses of the management style of women entrepreneurs.

THE BRISTOL STUDY: 1987-9

I identified twenty successful, well-established businesses run by women in Bristol. The criteria for selection were that the business must have been initiated and managed by a woman and not, for example, by a husband and wife team, that there had to be a minimum of four people being managed, and that the business had proved viable.

The businesses studied included women's co-operatives, sole traders and partnerships. The numbers of staff employed ranged from four to four hundred and fifty, and the types of business from employment agencies, financial services and large scale catering organizations to an engineering factory and a clothing manufacturer. It is interesting to note that these flourishing companies were often largely unknown in the city. The owners' ages varied from 25 to over 50.

My interview approach was semi-structured. All the entrepreneurs were asked the same open questions concerning their reasons for starting the business, their previous history, and their views and self-perceptions of their own style of management. Through a content analysis of the data, similarities and differences became apparent. For resource reasons I was unable to conduct an observational study of the women in action. I did, however, discuss with employees their perception of the management style, to see if there was corroboration of the owners' assertions.

The women owners were all intrigued and sometimes flattered that their views should be valued and considered. For most, this was the first time that they had considered their methods and values. Only one had attended any courses or read any management theories. Their responses were, therefore, original and expressed in their own terms.

THE MINERVA MATRIX

As a title and focus of my research, and also to give some needed emphasis to the undervalued and often unknown qualities and abilities of women, I went back to classical roots to adopt the goddess of wisdom, the Roman Minerva (Athena in Greece). I was later surprised to find that the same idea was occurring to other writers. Whitmont (1983) selected Pallas Athene as the inspiration for the career woman currently vulnerable in male dominated organizations and Charles Handy (1985) featured Athena as task-centred, a problem-solver; people with her style were those who value creativity, enthusiasm, joint commitment, and team work, seeing individuals as 'resourceful humans rather than human resources'.

REASONS FOR STARTING THE BUSINESS

Contrary to other research which has suggested that the main reasons which cause women to set up their own businesses are their frustration at the lack of opportunities or of promotion in established companies, the key motivators in Bristol were:

(a) *Survival* after a personal crisis or change of situation. 'Survival is basic to the female' (Rosemary Bugden, Interlink, a national parcel transport company). Ian Cunningham refers to this reactive factor associated with women entrepreneurs as follows:

> Essentially, they are reacting to an unsatisfactory situation and starting a company is often the best way of dispensing with the problem. Other variables in a woman's decision-making process include limited career and employment prospects, a lack of suitable qualifications, and the need to fit work hours around the home and family.
>
> (Clutterbuck and Devine 1987: 136)

For example, Sarah Squires of Kidstuff, a children's clothing manufacturing company, found herself needing to support three children with insufficient capital to continue her professional studies in law, and wondering 'what can I do?' (see also Jones this volume).
(b) *Dissatisfaction with the way men were running business* and the feeling that they could do better. 'Men are hopeless at business' (Diane Miller, Licensed Conveyancing Agent). 'Small engineering companies were shambolic' (Sally Jane Coode of Polamco Engineering).
(c) Realizing that there was *a gap in the market*. 'I saw the potential in silk flowers' (Sue Burt, Sabrina Vallis, florists). 'I couldn't find any good dungarees for my kids' (Sarah Squires, Kidstuff).

(d) *The satisfaction of making their own decisions*, something all the women found comparatively easy. 'Women are more decisive than men – they just waffle' (Diane Miller). Christine Mann, Mann and James, Chartered Accountants, left business after getting tired of the fact that 'no decisions were being made. Decisions were left to one person who waffled.'

(e) *Challenge*. This was the chief spur for most women, and remains the main motivator, together with enjoyment and fun. 'I wouldn't work unless it was for fun' (Rosemary Bugden). Women stated that they would stop working at the same pace if it stopped being enjoyable. Interestingly enough, only two entrepreneurs found their work stressful.

PREVIOUS EXPERIENCE

Previous research has highlighted the fact that most women start businesses with no real experience behind them (Clutterbuck and Devine 1987; Lessem 1986). This was true in the Bristol study for all except those women specializing in financial, personnel or legal matters. In these areas a sound background had been established before the launch into independence. All the rest positively triumph in this initial ignorance. 'I muddled along . . . I didn't know anything' (Sue Burt, Sabrina Vallis). 'No experience at all . . . I've blundered into things all my life' (Rosemary Bugden, Interlink). 'I've never seen inside anyone else's factory. I don't know how they work!' (Sarah Squires, Kidstuff).

This has been labelled the 'pioneer approach', the behaviour similar to that of 'immigrants who make up their own rules for the game' (Pinchot 1985: 57). There are similarities with two well-known British entrepreneurs, Anita Roddick and Richard Branson. They do not feel they are doing anything special, they do not know the rules, and have a sense of anarchy in wanting to break any existing rules that do not appeal.

Natasha Josefowitz (1980) summed up this approach in the following terms: pioneers needed, terrain uncharted, environment frequently hostile, sustenance meagre or non-existent, climate adverse, results uncertain, end of journey not in sight.

Gunnilla Steen, from Sweden, addressed this issue at the European Women's Management Development Conference held in Brighton in 1987. She pointed out that women managers 'are in a foreign culture', and for a real demonstration of their strengths need 'a critical mass for support'.

QUALITIES AND STRENGTHS

Women entrepreneurs in the USA have been attributed with possessing 'a well-honed sense of self' (Noble 1986: 33). It is interesting to see the qualities the Bristol entrepreneurs claim as theirs and as particularly female.

First and foremost, all believe strongly that women, but only a few men, have the ability to keep a lot of balls in the air at once. 'Men have tunnel vision' (Caroline Lloyd, Employment Agency) whereas women have a juggling ability, as can be seen in their management of a home and family (see Jones this volume). Being able to attend to all levels at once, make long-term and short-term decisions, distinguish crucial issues, and day to day detail is rated as vital to running a business.

Common sense is also highly valued. 'Although I've never been trained to do anything, I feel it's just common sense and I can't understand why people don't have it' (Sally Jane Coode, Polamco). Tact, the intuitive perception of people's feelings and reactions was believed to be indispensable to interpersonal relationships and a particular female strength. Humour and the ability to confess to making mistakes, which puts everyone on the same level, were felt to be very important. 'A man would play the Big White Chief' (Sue Sheppard, Employment Agency). Honesty, and an intrinsic determination for high standards rated as fundamental by these entrepreneurs, are not seen as solely female virtues, but all the women believed that stamina and sheer 'stickability' were particularly female attributes as, they felt, was good decision making. 'I can see solutions quickly. Decisions are things to be done, that's all' (Dee Hickling, Dish of the Day). Imagination and its expression as business flair, flexibility, and adaptability to change were deemed to be significant.

Sensitivity to others, listening to others, and sharing all facets of work and personal needs were highly valued. Women working in the Greenleaf Bookshop Co-operative spoke for many when they stated 'we believe we should bring the whole self to work'. Together with enthusiasm, a strong belief in what they are doing, emotional toughness to pull through the difficult times and, above all, a supportive non-hierarchical team of colleagues, were the main qualities which make up 90 per cent, which complements the 'madness' referred to by Daphne Gordon (MD of High Integrity Systems) who said 'You need 10 per cent of madness.'

MANAGEMENT STYLES

The style with which these women entrepreneurs set up and managed their businesses was not usually a preconsidered one, but developed out of the qualities identified above. Despite their lack of awareness of managerial theories, each woman had strong feelings about the organization of her business and the values to which it adhered and there were general similarities in approach. Ronnie Lessem (1985: 137) summarized his conclusions about female entrepreneurial management as relating to the ways in which a woman might run her own home. These 'are grafted into the business management', so that there is a loose hierarchy, with co-operation and a fluid style and she is 'less conscious of her authority and status'. Lessem perceived many entrepreneurs to have 'a personal, even maternal approach to customers and employees' caring deeply about the well-being of all staff. Steve Shirley, the founder of F International, claimed 'the same type of creativity which a mother feels for her children. In a way, I think of my company as a child; I created it, I moulded it, and now I have to leave it, to allow it to become independent.' This spirit of caring, involvement, and equality inspires the style in which the Bristol enterprises are run – even if one does proclaim herself to be 'a benevolent dictator'. Open communication and access, sharing of tasks and trust ensure that in crises people will be able to cover for each other, just as the owner will herself pitch in and scrub, butter bread, or unblock a drain. 'I never ask anyone to do anything I wouldn't do myself' (Shirley Knight, SRK Services). This seems to exemplify Lessem's statement (1985) that in business a woman has 'a wider and more flexible range of abilities than a male'.

All the entrepreneurs appreciated that with success their role would change, but all keep in firm touch with the basic day to day functions of the business. They pay scant attention to the labels and external trappings of success and feel that in this they do differ from most men who appear to need to demonstrate their status, – 'things like the size of their car matter more to a man' (Sally Jane Coode). She commented further that 'coming to business with no preconceived ideas, our organization is less structured. Everything is people in the end. We are able to get people to do things cheerfully.' Sue Burt, along with others, emphasized that apart from being the owner and the 'infuser of enthusiasm' her role was non-authoritarian. The team is equal, with personal and business problems alike being discussed. This sharing is important for those owners who are sole traders. Two of them had taken on male partners early in their initial expansion, but had found the relationship more destructive than useful, so were resolved not to repeat that experience. As sole traders, therefore, the sharing and pooling of ideas is valued by the owner, and a 'family feel' about the business is fundamental.

An important part of management style for many of the women is their pride and satisfaction not only in sharing the tasks and organization equally with others, but in consciously developing skills in their (largely) female work force and achieving a high degree of success. The women in the two Greenleaf co-operatives were particularly appreciative of this gain. Sue Burt, for example, encourages all her co-workers to feel that it is their business as well as hers, and to learn as much as she knows. Sarah Squires, who took the same approach, learned that 'people are good at everything, not just sewing, for example. . . . If you push, they get the skills . . . and develop.' She is particularly proud that her young female workers under 20 not only earn good money with her, but also gain the confidence to become house-owners.

This is the essence of the idea of transformational management which takes seriously the established definition of management as 'getting things done through other people' by positively encouraging ability and independence in staff. The power of managers is crucial. 'A manager: directs people or misdirects them; brings out what it is in them or stifles them; strengthens their integrity or corrupts them; trains them to stand upright and strong or deforms them' (Drucker 1984: 56).

The style of management practised by the women entrepreneurs may be summarized as: team-based with a strong 'family' feel; co-operative in nature; enabling' (i.e. developing potential in employees); dynamic and flexible in purpose, quickly reacting to variants internally and externally; rooted in desire for high standards and competitive products/services; medium risk taking; using intuitive decision-making; innovative; one preferring *win:win* strategies which result in satisfaction for all parties as against a *win:lose* where only one party gains.

Radha Chaganti (1986) compared the 'fit' of the seven strategic elements of enterprise management: shared values, strategies, structures, systems, staff, skills, and styles, and found that it was in the style of management in particular, that women differed from the male model. However, as some women in the Bristol study found, decisions have to be made concerning the maintaining of these valued qualities of management style when expansion makes this difficult. This will be discussed, briefly, below.

SOME COMMENTS ON BEING FEMALE

Many of the women in Bristol had experienced prejudice and difficulty when trying to obtain money from banks. 'Where is your husband?' was a frequent question, as were the condescending and sexist comments like 'Well, do your best, dear.' Sue Burt was constantly denied support by a bank which had been using her florist's services for years (see Koper this volume). One useful outcome of success was that it became much easier to deal with banks.

It does not occur to some women that they are any different. For example, Caroline Lloyd (Employment Agency) simply said 'I made it happen.' Others do think about it. 'Very singular, aren't we!' (Sue Burt). 'Being female may be a handicap in some areas, but to some women it appears empowering, it has a novelty factor . . . I can use it' (Dee Hickling). There can, however, be a feeling of 'loneliness at the top' (Brinion Heaton). A few join groups of like-minded business women such as the Bristol Business Ladies Club and Women in Enterprise, or happen to know other entrepreneurs or women managing in similar areas with whom to share problems. None of them read books on management – 'too busy', 'no time'.

TWO YEARS ON

In June 1989 I held a day conference to bring together those women who had contributed to my study. There had been developments. When we had met last, several women were considering new directions for their business and some of these had been put into operation. Dee Hickling, Avon Business Woman of the Year, had added to her chain of food shops and her various catering contracts by opening a restaurant of an innovative type for Bristol. She has also studied for the Diploma of Management Studies at Bristol Business School. The owners of Sugarcraft have decided to specialize and concentrate on manufacture. Jennifer Bryant Pearson of JBP consultants in PR, and also an award winner, has expanded. A new area of child care at work is developing alongside the Mary McCombe Secretarial Agency. Others, like Sabrina Vallis, are consolidating their position, or analysing their situation before taking the next step.

WHAT ADVICE DID THEY OFFER OTHER WOMEN ENTREPRENEURS?

I list below the kinds of advice they felt it helpful to offer:

- 'do hard research into your business area'
- 'seek good advice, particularly about finance'
- 'plan every detail, and the cost of everything – make sure you understand exactly what you are spending!'
- 'choose your name carefully – it can be your main advertising tool. It can explain what you do, but can also direct any blame on to you if your name is part of it'
- 'put effort into managing your time'
- 'plan time for yourself when it's possible, and avoid feeling guilty when you're not always at work'
- 'keep your confidence – and vision!'

REFLECTIVE COMMENTS ON THEIR MANAGEMENT

'I was in a dream world at the beginning. I never thought I'd fail.' Some women were amazed at the risks they had taken at the beginning and yet realized that compared with their current position, there had not been so very much to lose. Changing over from a personal, family style of organization to one of more delegation was felt to be a 'very painful' process. Expanding their business had meant that this became necessary, and feeling disloyal and even guilty at this stage was a common experience, as were sadness at losing the close common involvement with colleagues and being 'one of the team'. One or two, pointing out that difficult, unpalatable decisions had to be made, such as dealing with theft and staff dismissal, doubted whether 'open' management is ever as straightforward as it seems. They saw that accepting that one may not always be liked is an inevitable part of being a manager, or the boss. They also considered that it can be difficult for the team who have grown with the company to accept a change in the owner's style of management. When new staff arrive they perceive the manager to be 'more worldly-wise and knowledgeable' than they are, and so accept a certain division between them. One owner even recommended to others that they change their staff completely when the company develops to enable the altered management style to operate more smoothly and without resentment felt by the initial team.

All the entrepreneurs, however, agreed a good atmosphere was vital and that they enjoyed building up a loyal hard-core of staff who would respond to emergencies by working if necessary through the night. Identification with the business, camaraderie, and loyalty from staff were seen as valuable and valued assets for the owner/manager.

Finally they gave their views on management training. This they felt, after their experiences, to be necessary for those expanding their businesses. The particular areas where training was needed were in how expansion should take place, in which directions, when was the appropriate time to expand, what were the interpersonal skills required, and how were personnel matters to be dealt with.

CONCLUDING REMARKS

It has been claimed that the growth of women entrepreneurs is six times that of men, and their survival rate is equal (Clutterbuck and Devine 1987). Yet Hertz found that 'British women entrepreneurs are aloof . . . less visible and public than in America. It was a hard task finding them for my research' (Clutterbuck and Devine 1987). Women are still a novelty at the top of business hierarchies. It has to be noted that 90 per cent of women are in low paid, low skilled jobs and that the number of female managers in business has actually decreased since 1975. Yet management courses are increasingly taking women as students and in some British higher education institutions they make up as much as a half of those on such courses.

This indicates that not only should there be greater awareness by banks and other institutions of women's capabilities and potential, but that courses on management and small businesses need to adapt more positively to women. They should absorb recent explorations of androgenous-style management which incorporates both male and female strengths and of transformational management exemplified by most of the women entrepreneurs in Bristol. Women's strengths, qualities and preferred styles should be identified and included in the strategies offered by management.

There have been virtually no models for women as business owners. Women 'must be capable of developing in a vacuum' said Frances Pinto, owner of Pinto Publishing (Clutterbuck and Devine 1987). Women entrepreneurs are freer than women managers in traditional businesses, and can therefore be original and creative in their approach. They are, as we have seen from the findings of the Bristol Study, 'more concerned to maintain a balance between achieving and nurturing' while male entrepreneurs tend to follow 'an achievement model' (Devine and Clutterbuck 1985).

My research reveals the declared stances and functional preferences of some successful women entrepreneurs. It also echoes their own beliefs that, to quote Sue Burt, if women can succeed now against the odds, 'Women have to be bloody good!'

5 Women entrepreneurs and the granting of business credit

Gerda Koper

Ever since the 1960s the participation rate of women in the labour market has been increasing in The Netherlands. In 1960 only 22 per cent of the labour force consisted of women; by 1987 it was 38 per cent (Central Bureau voor de Statistiek [CBS] 1985). If we look only at married women, the increase is even more spectacular: in 1960 it was 7 per cent, in 1979, 25 per cent, and in 1987 it was 33 per cent (CBS 1985). Compared with other countries, however, the rate of married women in the labour market is still very small.

The most important factors that have contributed to the increase in the number of female employees are stagnating economic growth and the progressive emancipation of women. Because of the stagnation in economic growth and the subsequent decrease in wages at the beginning of the 1980s, women were forced to look for paid jobs in order to compensate for the decrease in family income. In addition, the women's movement has had a great influence on many women, which has led to an increase in female employees. Growing self-confidence in their own abilities among women, better accessibility to education, and the wish to be economically independent of their partner or husband stimulates women to look for paid jobs or to set up their own business (Koper and Vermunt 1988).

Although the number of women in the labour market is increasing, women mostly work part-time because of the unequal distribution of work at home, so that they are responsible for only 25 per cent of total hours worked. Furthermore, women with paid jobs are mainly found in jobs that are related to the work they do at home. They are still over-represented in occupations with educational, caring, and service-related characteristics. Apart from the fact that the work women do is mainly restricted to a few occupations, it is restricted also to jobs with few responsibilities, training facilities, or potential for promotion. Women are highly under-represented in managerial and supervisory jobs.

According to the Dutch government this unequal position of men and women in the labour market is anchored in Dutch society. There is the question of an unequal balance of power between men and women. The government admits that women, compared to men, have a disadvantaged position in the labour market. Moreover, it is acknowledged that a redistribution of paid and unpaid work between men and women is the way to remove the disadvantaged position of women. More women will have to participate in paid employment and more men will have to participate in unpaid work.

Part of the government's policy for achieving this redistribution is Affirmative Action (AA). The Netherlands has a legal basis for AA in the second EC directive on Equal Treatment, which emphasizes the use of AA when it is aimed at reducing a disadvantage for certain groups (De Rijk 1987). AA includes measures that are applied by government and industry to increase the number of women in the labour market on the one hand and on the other to create better promotion possibilities for women in organizations. The ultimate goal of AA is to attain proportional representation of women in the labour market in all jobs and on all levels in organizations.

In practice AA means that in advertisements, for example, only women are invited to apply for a certain post whereas inviting only men to apply is not allowed, and that in cases of candidates of equal suitability, women take precedence over men. AA also includes investigating why women do not apply for certain jobs. Not only can the image of certain jobs play an important role in discouraging them, but the educational qualifications required play a part. In fact in The Netherlands there are few women who have had a technical education and many are therefore unable to apply for jobs where such qualifications are specified. AA does not just relate to preferential treatment for individual women, it also includes the possibility that attention be given to sexual harassment and to the preconditions of employment such as day-care facilities, working hours, and special leave.

AA consists of measures appropriate to women who are looking for employment or who already have a paid job. So far the position of those women who seek to be self-employed has not been considered in terms of how useful or relevant AA measures are to them, or the possibility that potential female entrepreneurs may need different forms of AA.

The number of women entrepreneurs is increasing as a consequence of factors mentioned earlier, but there appears to be a large difference between women's participation rate in the labour market and that in business enterprises. One-third of those employed are female, while only one-sixth of all entrepreneurs are women. This seems to indicate that there are relatively more problems for women in setting up their own business than in finding paid jobs.

Koopman and Walvis (1986) point to a number of possible reasons that may be responsible for the under-representation of female entrepreneurs in The Netherlands. First, they argue that differential socialization is involved (see Jones in this volume). Characteristics associated with entrepreneurship are 'ambition', 'self-confidence', 'resolution', 'assertiveness'. These characteristics are usually not attributed or ascribed to women and are usually not encouraged in women in The Netherlands. Second, they maintain that the education, training, and work experience of women are often not adequate for starting up their own business. Women frequently work in paid employment in capacities such as routine administrative work that are not suitable for starting a business. They do not generally have specific professional training or enough work experience to form the necessary basis for starting a business. Third, although some changes in traditional gender roles have taken place, these have not led to a substantial redistribution of housework (Emler and Abrams 1990). In many cases, therefore, women have to combine running a business and taking care of their family. This may mean that women entrepreneurs have to adapt or restrict their entrepreneurial activities (see Epstein this volume). In the worst instances the combination of entrepreneurship and domestic labour is not possible at all because of a lack of day-care facilities for children.

Finally, Koopman and Walvis see the most important problem for women who want to start their own business as that of finance. Although finance is a problem for potential entrepreneurs in general, research in The Netherlands has indicated that it is a much bigger problem for women than for men. Female entrepreneurs appear to have more difficulties in getting business credit from banks than men and the same authors indicate that, both from the reactions of entrepreneurs as well as contacts with banks, women are taken less seriously than men when presenting their business plans. Veenstra (1986) also reports complaints from women concerning their treatment by banks. These complaints include the reluctance of bank employees to give information, and to take seriously their business plans and requests for credit to start up a business. Research by Statistisch Kwalitatie Industrieel Marktonderzoek (SKIM 1985) showed that the dissatisfaction of women who want to start a business is mainly directed at those they contact in banks, and that female entrepreneurs say they continue to face a great deal of misunderstanding from banks.

GRANTING BUSINESS CREDIT

Given the research findings referred to above about the difficulties women reported they had in obtaining credit, Koper and Vermunt undertook a study which aimed to get a clearer picture of the specific problems women meet. It became obvious that the reasons for these difficulties were by no means unambiguous. The procedures for the granting of business credit are not just technical. While financial and economic aspects play a part, the processes of social interaction between entrepreneur and bank employee are of major significance. In our study we distinguished a number of aspects as having an influence on these procedures.

Objective aspects

These correspond to objectively perceived facts such as specific information concerning the business and the personal aspects of the entrepreneur. For example, *the potential market profitability of the business*, the choice of a particular market sector, and the age, work experience, education, and capital assets of the entrepreneur. We found several objective aspects that may negatively influence the process of granting credit to female entrepreneurs.

Among these were included *potential discontinuity* and *sector choice*. In The Netherlands the general belief prevails that women stop working after having their first child. In reality, many women entrepreneurs with children are responsible for both their business and taking care of their families. Banking institutions, however, assume in advance that women entrepreneurs will have a *discontinuous* career pattern. The traditional segregation between male and female occupations in the labour market appears to exist also when women and men choose to start a business. Eighty-seven per cent of women are working in service-related industries, while 12.5 per cent have a job in the industrial manufacturing sector. According to research carried out by SKIM (1985) 46 per cent of female entrepreneurs are working in personal and social services, 29 per cent in the food, clothing and leather industries, and 25 per cent in retail and repair businesses. Relatively few women entrepreneurs (9.6 per cent) start in manufacturing or craft occupations. This research concludes that businesses started by women are mostly to be found in areas which reflect the caring functions of their everyday, private lives. This sector preference may be one reason why banks are reluctant to grant business credit to women. Retail, catering, and certain service-related areas are considered to carry a high risk for banks, because of the excessive penetration into these areas, low family income, small turnover and small profits, so that any investment hardly renders adequate revenue.

Subjective aspects

Subjective aspects have no correspondence with objective facts, and include opinions, interpretations, evaluations of objective aspects, and stereotypic ideas about sex-roles. We grouped those aspects that may negatively influence the granting of credit to women entrepreneurs under two headings, *the missing frame of reference*, and *sex-stereotypical assessments*. In The Netherlands few women are found in managerial positions. In granting business credit not only are objective facts considered but the personal qualities of the entrepreneur are also assessed. The expectations about the personality and behaviour of a potential entrepreneur are usually based by credit granters on the clients they know, who are mainly male entrepreneurs. Consequently, those in a position to grant credit do not have a frame of reference within which female entrepreneurship is well defined.

Sex stereotypes have been defined as 'Consensual beliefs about the differing characteristics of men and women' (Rosenkrantz et al. 1968: 287). Research on sex stereotypes in The Netherlands, as elsewhere, has shown that different characteristics are attributed to women from those attributed to men (Wegner and Vallacher 1977). It has been argued that there is a great deal of consensus on the correspondence of certain characteristics with personality types (Hampson 1982). This appears to be the case among bank employees who assess male and female entrepreneurs in The Netherlands.

The implicit personality theory held by people socialized in Dutch society concerning 'the entrepreneur' together with sex-stereotyping may have an important influence on their business credit granting behaviour toward women. Entrepreneurship is associated with characteristics such as 'resolution', 'ambition' and 'perseverance'. These characteristics are not usually attributed to women (Koopman and Walvis 1986). Consequently women entrepreneurs are viewed with scepticism and the qualities of female entrepreneurs viewed prejudicially. It is not surprising that those in banking institutions react more reluctantly in granting business credits to women than to men.

ENTREPRENEURS' PERCEPTIONS

Besides the objective and subjective aspects involved in decisions to grant or withhold credit, it is important to investigate how the entrepreneur perceives the treatment of his or her request for credit by the bank. In the case of the credit granting process there is an interaction between on the one hand the procedures applied by the bank and the bank employee's expectations, opinions and interpretations, and on the other hand the entrepreneur's request for credit and the expectations and interpretations which surround this.

In our research we tried to develop a better understanding of the ways in which women applying for credit to start-up a business are treated by banks, and investigated the constraints they meet in getting this kind of credit. We were interested in seeking ways in which the constraints could be reduced and looked in particular at possible AA measures.

THE RESEARCH DESIGN

Subjects were recruited in two ways – by advertisements placed in entrepreneurial magazines, and from a population of 500 entrepreneurs drawn from the trade register of Chambers of Commerce in seven cities. The advertisement asked new entrepreneurs who had experience of applying to banks for credit to participate; the others were approached by letter and asked to complete a short preliminary questionnaire.

In total 288 responses were received. After eliminating those who did not meet the criteria or were unable or unwilling to participate, 76 entrepreneurs, 37 female and 39 male remained. Forty of these, 19 women and 21 men, reported a positive experience, meaning that they got the finance they requested, whereas 36 had a negative experience. Equal numbers of women and men therefore reported their experience as negative. Data were collected by means of a semi-structured questionnaire on the objective and subjective aspects of the respondents' perceptions of the process.

In addition to the entrepreneurs, commercial bank employees (32 men and 2 women) were interviewed using a semi-structured questionnaire. All handled requests for business credit in business start-up for three (big) banks in The Netherlands that account for about 50 per cent of all such requests made.

Before the interview, the bank employees were asked to judge a business plan drawn-up by an expert. This was partly based on a real plan and was in part fictitious. The bank employees were told that they would be asked questions about how they judged the plan. In this way we could achieve a better understanding of those aspects they considered relevant in dealing with granting credit to start-up businesses. The business plans were presented to half of the respondents as being drawn up by two women and to the others as drawn up by two men. Finally, in order to determine the importance of stereotypical judgements both bank employees and entrepreneurs were presented with thirty-seven characteristics and asked to judge these in terms of their desirability for potential entrepreneurs and on whether they considered them to be masculine, feminine or neutral.

RESEARCH FINDINGS

As we argued above, women who want to start in business meet with more obstacles than men in getting business credit from banks. In this, a number of objective and subjective aspects appear to play an important part.

According to the bank employees we interviewed women, more often than men, start-up businesses that are non-profitable. These are businesses in marginal and home-oriented sectors (such as second-hand clothing). No salaries can be paid but expenses are covered. Because such businesses are not commercially attractive bank employees indicated that they were cautious in granting business credit.

In our study women entrepreneurs were strongly represented in retail and clothing wholesale and catering, (54 per cent) and in service-related sectors (35 per cent), and to a much lesser extent in industrial branches (11 per cent) (see Johnson and Storey this volume). Men exhibited a somewhat different pattern. They were also strongly represented in retail clothing and catering (49 per cent), but almost three times as many, compared to the women, were in industrial branches (31 per cent). Twenty per cent were in service related businesses. The bank employees indicated that they were not eager to grant credit to entrepreneurs who want to start a business in highly risky branches, where there was a strong possibility of bankruptcy.

Women choose branches that are easily accessible to them. They become coffee-shop owners, or set up clothing shops. Often they lack the professional education and have too little experience of other sectors to do otherwise. Male entrepreneurs, in addition to locating their businesses in the same sectors as women, also start up building companies, transport services, metal or machine industries. In general these differences reflect the segregation found in the labour market.

Requests for credit that do not exceed $12,500 are according to the bank employees nonprofitable from the bank's point of view because the time they take to process is not justified financially by the profit they make. Most of the women entrepreneurs in our survey indicated that their requests for credit were under $12,500 whereas most of the men made requests which exceeded this figure. Of the thirty-six requests for credit which were rejected, fourteen fell into the range of $5,500 to $12,500. The initial capital of women was rather low, mainly not exceeding $5,000, but for men it was often higher, ranging between $5,500 and $12,500.

Expectations about entrepreneurship and ideas about the sex-roles of men and women influence the granting of business credit. The bank employees hold traditional views on the sexual division of labour, expecting that the husband works full time and earns the family income and the wife runs the home and looks after the children. This was demonstrated by the different questions they were asked when requesting credit. Women entrepreneurs are asked to show their spouse's pay-slip or, if they were unmarried, evidence of a financial guarantee from their father; men are not. Women, but not men, are asked whether they have children or whether they plan to have children in the future and are expected to produce a solution about how they intend to run a business in combination with bringing up children. This combination often forces women to take up part-time employment. According to the bank employees a *real* entrepreneur works full time or even more than full time. Most bank employees are of the opinion that starting a business in combination with bringing up children cannot be done. Some of them are even cautious about granting credit to women at all, because in their eyes the risks of marriage and pregnancy make women unsuitable.

The judgements of bank employees and entrepreneurs on which characteristics were desirable in new entrepreneurs are given in Table 5.1. The employees and entrepreneurs were also asked to categorize those characteristics in terms of their masculinity, femininity or neutral status. There was a high degree of agreement between the

Table 5.1 New entrepreneurs: characteristics by desirability and sex-typing*

	Masculine	Feminine	Neutral
Desirable	Forceful	Attentive	Active
	Rational	Co-operative	Daring
	Self-conscious	Tactful	Improvizational
	Ambitious	Understanding	Serious
	Resolute		Versatile
			Inquisitive
			Flexible
			Perseverance
			Enthusiastic
			Creative
			Dynamic
			Independent
			Incorruptible
			Imaginative
			Logical thinking
			Purposeful
Undesirable	Dominant	Emotional	Absent-minded
	Reckless	Gentle	
		Irresolute	
Neutral	Jovial	Spontaneous	Attractive
	Formal	Sensitive	
		Intuitive	

*The characteristics are drawn from an instrument for assessing sex-stereotypical judgements (van Vianen et al. 1986)

entrepreneurs and the bank employees on both these judgements. The most desirable characteristics for starting a business were considered to be perseverance, ambition, resolution and self-awareness. Three of these were judged to be masculine and the other, perseverance, as neutral. However, the entrepreneurs who were interviewed, both men and women, considered themselves to possess these characteristics (see Table 5.2).

PERCEIVED TREATMENT

The judgements on the business plans we presented did not show any relation between the supposed gender of the author and the granting of credit. However, the interviews with the employees indicated that men and women were treated differently.

There was a large inter-employee difference in the way credit requests are judged and treated. This is most apparent from the

Table 5.2 Entrepreneurs' views of their rating on the most desirable characteristics – average scores*

Characteristic	Women	Men
Perseverance	1.58	1.42
Ambition	2.00	1.96
Resolution	1.72	1.67
Self-awareness	2.45	2.19

*5 point scale: 5 = not at all applicable to myself; 1 = very much applicable to myself

judgements about motivation for starting a business, market research, and financial aspects of the business plans. Judgements concerning these are at times contradictory. One employee claimed that entrepreneurs were only concerned with making money and did not have the interest of their business at heart. Another employee remarked that the entrepreneurs were too idealistic (which is considered a weak point) and not at all interested in making money.

Some employees judged the financial structure of the plan as reasonable or even as very good, while others judged the same financial structure as inadequate. There appeared to be no relation between judgements on the business plan and granting or not granting of credit. When a business plan is judged as good credit is not automatically granted. Conversely, entrepreneurs with a business plan judged negatively are not necessarily denied credit. The variation between employees means that when trying a second or third bank for credit, the chances are equal, or even higher, of getting it. Obtaining business credit seems like playing roulette.

The way in which entrepreneurs perceive their treatment by banks is highly coloured by whether or not they are granted credit. A negative experience results in a negative evaluation and conversely a positive experience results in a positive evaluation. Female entrepreneurs whose experience had been negative were more (strongly) of the view that they had not been taken seriously by bank employees than male entrepreneurs were ($F = 7.170$; $df = 1.34$; $p<.01$). Bank employees denied that they treated women differently or more critically than men. According to them, all credit requests are tested against objective financial and economic aspects, and women and men have an equal chance of getting business credit.

Bank employees do, however, admit that the personality of the potential entrepreneur and their abilities eventually constitute the most important factors in deciding whether to grant credit, so the subjective aspects appear to have more relevance.

CONCLUSIONS

The results from this study indicate that at present banks are not applying affirmative action measures with respect to female entrepreneurs. On the contrary, the procedural criteria they formulate make it harder for women to set up their own business. Banks are service companies which are profit oriented, and affirmative action seems to them to be in conflict with their main objective.

However, affirmative action does not mean that women who are definitely unfit for entrepreneurship or who have business plans that are clearly inadequate have to be given business credit. It means that an incentive programme has to be developed, directed at (potential) female entrepreneurs, in which both banks and the government participate. The main objective of this programme would be to contribute to the reduction of the restrictions women meet in starting up businesses in general and when requesting business credit in particular. This incentive programme has to be a concern of the government initially if women are to have the opportunity to utilize their full potential.

Such a programme would include an important educational element. Women have not so far received education aimed at motivating them for entrepreneurship. As a consequence women choose technical training less often than men, and hardly ever participate in training programmes for entrepreneurs. Incentives to motivate women to take up technical education and training are required. Education and training can also question and try to alter existing sex-role stereotypes. Starting up a business in Dutch society is still associated with characteristics like 'resolution', 'ambition', 'self-confidence' and 'perseverance' which are seen largely as male attributes. Changing the image of 'the entrepreneur' will involve paying attention to the capacities and qualities women have (see Vokins, this volume). Women have their own way of managing a business. They often manage their business more democratically than men, they think less hierarchically, they admit they are wrong more easily so that decision making processes proceed faster. Moreover, they are more sociable than men are, so they are able to motivate their employees more effectively. This is a Human Interest oriented style of management (Peereboom 1988). It is argued that this is a more efficient and more determined way of managing a business (Peters and Waterman 1982; Hughey and Gelman 1986).

In addition, we would include characteristics like 'creativeness', 'intuition' and 'expertise' as essential to an entrepreneur, and these are frequently thought of as female characteristics. By defining these characteristics as feminine it may be possible to create a more differentiated approach to entrepreneurship.

However, without creating more day-care facilities and tax relief for domestic help and child care, a programme aimed at stimulating female entrepreneurship is likely to fail. Female entrepreneurs in The Netherlands are not entitled to antenatal or maternity benefits. Since these women are, so to speak, having their babies 'behind the counter', legal changes are needed to secure social benefits for them. Additional provisions will be necessary in the incentive programme for women who have few capital resources of their own to start up a business. It is possible, for example, to set a lower rate of interest for initial capital in the case of State-guaranteed credits and to design and support specific financial arrangements that stimulate female entrepreneurship.

The contribution of banks to such an incentive programme must take account of their main objective, which is to make profits. However, banks are starting to realize that the number of female entrepreneurs is increasing and, consequently, so is the number of female clients of financial institutions. Women employed by banks are hardly ever concerned with granting credit to entrepreneurs. The men who carry out this function, as we argued earlier, have no appropriate frame of reference where women are concerned. They have little, if any, experience of women in higher managerial positions or even in the same job as themselves. So their expectations and interpretations are based mainly on the clients they know, who are almost exclusively male. This leads to what may be termed the 'psychological resistance' which many women starting up in business meet when they request credit from banks. As a result these women think that they will never be able to prove themselves in what they call 'that male dominated bank culture'. This process of interaction is the cause of many women being disinclined to use bank loans, and instead to try to borrow money from friends or family or to give up their plans for setting up a business altogether.

It seems in the interest of all the parties concerned, both in terms of commercial considerations and improving the service to female entrepreneurs, that more women bank employees need to become involved in the work of granting credit for businesses. More generally, these procedures could be designed more objectively, by ensuring that credit requests are judged by at least two independent persons or a committee of men and women. They would hear the entrepreneur's case and reach a decision. Such a change in the procedure would, in our view, be of benefit particularly to women.

Female entrepreneurs are as good as and sometimes better than men (Amsterdam-Rotterdam Bank 1988). For instance, they become bankrupt less often (Van Eijndhoven 1986). But female entrepreneurs are of the opinion that they are not taken, or at least taken less, seriously by banks than men.

Entrepreneurship can be a considerable burden for women, especially in combination with bringing up children. Female entrepreneurs may choose to work part time because of this, but it does not mean it cannot be done. It may give small financial gain at the start of the business, but this tells us little about management abilities and it does not have to involve extra financial risks for the bank (SKIM/EIM 1988). An incentive programme in which banks participate can be successful only if the banks take a more positive attitude toward female entrepreneurship. Clinging strictly to norms, procedures and ratios which are based on 'standard business management' results in discrimination and leads to the unjust refusal of business credit to women.

6 Male and female entrepreneurs and their businesses
A comparative study

Steve Johnson and David Storey

INTRODUCTION

Women comprise 25 per cent of the self-employed population in Great Britain, a proportion which has been steadily increasing since the early 1980s. Clearly, not all self-employed people can be described as small business owners or 'entrepreneurs'. For example, around two-thirds of the self-employed population do not employ any other people besides themselves (Creigh et al. 1986). However, it would seem reasonable to assume that the level of small business ownership amongst women is increasing at a similar rate to the growth of self-employment. An analysis of General Household Survey (GHS) data by Curran and Burrows (1988a) suggests that around 25 per cent of small business owners in 1984 were women. Despite the obvious numerical importance in the small business sector of firms which are owned and controlled by women, and despite the growing interest in the role of women in the labour market more generally (see for example Hunt 1988), there has been surprisingly little research into women and self-employment/small business ownership. There has been even less work which has compared the characteristics and background of male and female business owners and/or the characteristics and performance of their businesses. This chapter presents some results from a survey of 298 small businesses conducted in 1985 and a follow-up survey of 184 of these firms which were still in existence at the end of 1988. Although the survey was not designed specifically to facilitate a comparison between male- and female-owned businesses, sixty-seven of the firms which participated in the 1985 survey were owned and managed by women, of whom fifty-one had originally founded their firms. This provides a reasonable basis upon which to undertake comparisons between male- and female-run businesses.

PREVIOUS WORK ON FEMALE ENTREPRENEURS

The dearth of UK research into female entrepreneurship has been noted elsewhere (see Allen and Truman, this volume). The volume of such research in the US has been somewhat higher (Watkins and Watkins 1982), and the US Small Business Administration regularly includes a report on trends in female business ownership in its Annual Reports to the President. This brief review will concentrate upon the research which has been undertaken in the UK.

There have been, to the authors' knowledge, only three major studies into female entrepreneurship in the UK during the 1980s (Watkins and Watkins 1984; Goffee and Scase 1985; Carter and Cannon 1988a). In addition, detailed analyses of the Labour Force Survey (Creigh et al. 1986) and the GHS (Curran and Burrows 1988a) have produced some comparisons of the demographic characteristics of self-employed men and women. The studies by Goffee and Scase (1985) and by Carter and Cannon (1988a) focus specifically upon female-owned businesses and do not attempt to compare the experiences of men and women. Thus, although these studies provide useful insights into the attitudes, motivations, and problems faced by women entrepreneurs, the lack of any control group of male-owned business in either of these studies precludes any comparative analysis. Watkins and Watkins (1984) compare the characteristics and background of a group of forty-nine female-owned and forty-three male-owned businesses. They discovered several differences between male and female small business owners. The women were significantly less likely than the men to be married, and the age distribution of women founders was found to be bi-modal, with significant concentrations in the 25-35 and 55-60 age ranges. This compares with the age distribution for male founders, which was found to be more evenly distributed around a mean of about 39 years. The distribution of educational qualifications was also found to vary considerably between male and female business owners, with men being significantly more likely than women to possess some form of professional qualification. Watkins and Watkins (1984) also found that women business founders were less likely than men to have been involved in an activity directly related to their current business venture immediately prior to start-up. The study concludes by suggesting that the backgrounds, motivations and experiences of women entrepreneurs differ substantially from those of men, with women being much less likely than men to have had relevant prior training and/or experience, leading women into forming businesses in activities and at times which may not appear to be entirely 'logical' when compared with the start-up process which is followed by the typical male entrepreneur.

The Labour Force Survey (LFS) (Creigh et al. 1986) indicates that self-employed women are marginally less likely than their male equivalents to employ other people, and are far more likely than men to be involved in distribution, hotels, catering, repairs, and other services. Self-employed women tend to work shorter hours than do their male counterparts, but there appear to be no major differences in the age distribution of the two groups. Finally, almost 44 per cent of self-employed women fall into the 'managerial' occupational category, as compared with 29 per cent of men. This difference can largely be explained by the large proportion of male construction workers who are classified as being self-employed. A very similar picture of the age and sectoral distribution and hours worked of male and female business owners is painted by the analysis of GHS data by Curran and Burrows (1988a). It also demonstrated that female small business owners (defined as those with between one and twenty-five employees) are much less likely than males to hold formal educational, professional or vocational qualifications.

The picture which results from this brief review of UK research is mixed, and can certainly not be described as conclusive. Although a great deal of information on the demographic characteristics of the self-employed can be gleaned from sources such as the LFS and the GHS, this tells us very little about the characteristics and performance of the businesses which are run by these people. The survey research which has been conducted to date has either concentrated solely upon female-run businesses, or has compared only the start-up process and not the subsequent performance of businesses run by men and women. This chapter attempts to fill some of the gaps which exist in our knowledge by utilizing a survey database which covers all types of small businesses, and which examines both the start-up process, the key characteristics, and the subsequent performance of the surveyed businesses.

THE 1985 AND 1988 OSG SURVEYS

The results presented here are derived from two surveys, the first conducted in 1985 and a follow-up survey which took place at the end of 1988.[1] A total of 298 small, independently owned firms were interviewed in 1985 in six selected labour market areas throughout Great Britain (London, Glasgow, Corby, Teesside, Reading and Morecambe/Lancaster). The interviews were conducted by a combination of personal and telephone techniques, and covered the start-up process of the firm, the characteristics and background of the founder of the firm and/or its 'chief executive', current and past levels of employment, brief financial details, and expectations about future performance. The follow-up was a telephone survey in which all of the 1985 respondents who could be traced at the end of 1988 were asked about any changes which had taken place in their businesses since 1985, with a particular emphasis upon employment change.

The results reported here are derived from an analysis of the answers given by the 226 respondents who claimed to be both an owner and a manager of the business. Of these 226 respondents, 162 claimed also to have been involved in the founding of the firm when it was first established. Table 6.1 summarizes the positions of the respondents in their businesses. Just under half of the respondents were sole owners of their businesses, and 44 per cent were in partnership with other people. The remaining 8 per cent were shareholders in and/or directors of limited companies. The only noticeable difference between the male and female respondents is that females are marginally more likely to be partners and less likely than males to be shareholders and/or directors. Unfortunately, it is not possible to distinguish those businesses which are run by women in partnership with other women from those in which men (often the husband of the respondent) are involved, as no further information was collected about partners. In the subsequent analyses, results are presented for all firms, and for sole owners only, in order to facilitate comparisons of like with like.

Table 6.2 illustrates the sectoral composition of the surveyed firms. The sample is broadly representative of the small business population as a whole, as indicated by the figures on registrations for Value Added Tax (VAT) (Ganguly 1985). There is a clear difference in the sectors in which men and women owner/managers are operating their businesses. Women are heavily concentrated in the retail, catering, and other services sectors, whilst men operate significantly more manufacturing, construction, and transport firms than women. These differences are particularly noticeable amongst women who are the sole owners of their businesses, of whom 88 per cent were in retailing, catering or other services. This picture of the sectoral distribution of firms is what might have been expected on the basis of the figures on the sectoral distribution of self-employed people (Creigh et al. 1986). Clearly, this mismatch between the sectoral distributions of male- and female-owned businesses complicates any analysis of other differences between them, making it more difficult to disentangle the sectoral

Table 6.1 Position in firm of owner/manager by gender

	Male	Female	All firms
Sole owner of business			
No. of respondents	77	31	108
% of respondents	49	47	48
Partner in business			
No. of respondents	65	32	97
% of respondents	41	49	44
Shareholder/director etc.			
No. of respondents	15	3	18
% of respondents	10	5	8
No answer			
No. of respondents	2	1	3
% of respondents	1	1	1
Total no. of respondents	159	67	226

Source: 1985 and 1988 OSG Surveys

Table 6.2 Sectoral distribution of sample by gender of owner/manager

	All firms			Sole owners only		
	Male	Female	All	Male	Female	All
	(column percentages in bold)					
Manufacturing	31	6	37	15	1	6
	20	**9**	**16**	**20**	**3**	**15**
Construction, transport and	32	2	34	13	2	15
motor trade	**20**	**3**	**15**	**17**	**6**	**14**
Retailing and wholesaling	53	30	83	23	17	40
	31	**46**	**36**	**30**	**55**	**37**
Professional services	11	1	12	7	1	8
	7	**2**	**5**	**9**	**3**	**7**
Catering	11	11	22	5	3	8
	7	**16**	**10**	**7**	**10**	**7**
Other services	24	16	40	14	7	21
	15	**24**	**18**	**18**	**23**	**19**
Base (= 100%)	159	67	226	77	31	108

Source: 1985 and 1988 OSG Surveys

effect from any possible gender-related influences. In order to minimize this problem, the results which are presented in the remain-

Table 6.3 Date of firm start-up by gender of founder – retail, catering and other services

	All firms			Sole owners only		
	Male	Female	All	Male	Female	All
	(column percentages)					
Between 1980 and 1985	42	46	44	42	45	43
Between 1975 and 1980	29	21	26	23	30	26
Between 1960 and 1975	18	26	21	23	25	24
Before 1960	11	8	10	13	–	8
Base (= 100%)	55	39	94	31	20	51

Source: 1985 and 1988 OSG Surveys

Table 6.4 Age of founder at time of start-up by gender of founder – retail, catering and other services

	All firms			Sole owners only		
	Male	Female	All	Male	Female	All
	(column percentages)					
Under 30	43	26	36	41	22	34
Between 30 and 39	31	47	38	28	44	34
Between 40 and 49	22	24	22	28	33	30
50 or older	4	3	4	3	–	2
Base (= 100%)	51	34	85	29	18	47

Source: 1985 and 1988 OSG Surveys

der of this chapter refer only to the retailing, catering, and other services sectors, in which the vast majority of female-owned businesses are to be found.

THE START-UP PROCESS

This section examines the start-up processes of the surveyed firms and compares the characteristics and background of male and female founders, their sources of start-up finance and the problems which they faced in their first years of operation. Table 6.3 illustrates that the dates of start-up of the male- and female-owned businesses are broadly similar, with businesses owned solely by women being, on average, of slightly shorter duration than those started by men.

Very clear differences emerge in the age distributions of the founders at the time of start-up, as can be seen in Table 6.4.

The male entrepreneurs are, on average, much younger than their female counterparts, with 43 per cent being under 30 years old at the time of start-up. In contrast, only 26 per cent of women, and only 22 per cent of female sole owners, were in the youngest age bracket at the time of start-up. Women founders are particularly heavily concentrated in the 30 to 50 age range. This contrasts sharply with the results obtained by Watkins and Watkins (1984) who found that the average age of women founder was less than that of men.

Table 6.5 confirms the views expressed by Watkins and Watkins (1984) and supported by the evidence presented by Curran and Burrows (1988a) that women business owners are less likely than their male counterparts to hold formal qualifications (with this difference being statistically significant for sole owners), but there appears to be no significant difference in the propensity of men and women business owners to undertake relevant training in the early stages of the business. Women founders are marginally less likely than men to have had prior experience of business ownership and/or self-employment, and are slightly more likely to have been unemployed (or under threat of unemployment) immediately prior to starting their businesses. Male sole owners are significantly more likely than women to have operated their business on a part time basis prior to starting full time, and men and women founders are equally likely to have sought assistance from Government or similar agencies immediately prior to start-up or during the first year of operation.

The sources of finance which were utilized by the firm founders are shown in Table 6.6. The importance of personal saving for all founders is clearly illustrated, with 76 per cent of men and 69 per cent of women mentioning this source. The second most mentioned source of start-up finance was that of clearing banks, which were mentioned by 46 per cent of all founders. However, loans or overdrafts from clearing banks were mentioned more frequently by men than by women founders. This result lends some support to the argument that women who wish to start a business are discriminated against by (mainly male) bank managers. However, the responses to a further question which asked whether respondents had attempted (and failed) to obtain other sources of start-up finance revealed no significant differences between the experiences of men and women. This does not mean, of course, that women do not suffer from discrimination on the part of the banks (see Koper this volume). It merely illustrates that women who have successfully set up in business do not appear to have suffered such

Table 6.5 Characteristics of new firm founders by gender – retail, catering and other services

	All firms			Sole owners only		
	Female	All	Male	Female	All	Male
	(column percentages)					
Holds formal qualifications	47	35	42	61	25	47*
Received training	18	25	21	19	10	16
Previously self-employed	6	3	5	3	6	4
Previously owned a business	18	8	14	19	10	16
Unemployed prior to start-up	33	40	36	32	40	35
Business was previously part-time occupation	15	4	11	21	–	13*
Sought help in early years	11	15	13	10	15	12
Base (= 100%)	55	40	95	31	20	51

Source: 1985 and 1988 OSG Surveys
* significant at the 5 per cent level

Table 6.6 Sources of start-up finance by gender of founder – retail, catering and other services

	All firms			Sole owners only		
	Male	Female	All	Male	Female	All
	(column percentages)					
Personal savings	76	69	73	70	67	69
House mortgage	8	11	9	10	11	10
Loans from friends or relations	9	17	12	10	22	15
Loan or overdraft from clearing bank	55	33	46	53	33	46
Redundancy money	2	3	2	3	–	2
Other sources	8	11	9	10	17	13
No. of sources mentioned (= 100%)	53	36	89	30	18	48

Source: 1985 and 1988 OSG Surveys
Note: Columns do not sum to 100 per cent because respondents could mention more than one source of finance

discrimination. The evidence is consistent with the argument that women are deterred from even seeking clearing bank finance, whether due to lack of confidence on the part of potential women entrepreneurs or to the fear of discrimination. We have, however, no way of

78 Women in business

Table 6.7 Problems faced in first year by gender of founder – retail, catering and other services

	All firms			Sole owners only		
	Male	Female	All	Male	Female	All
	(column percentages)					
Shortage of supplies	24	12	19	13	12	12
Shortage of skilled labour	17	15	16	12	–	7
High labour turnover	7	6	6	4	–	2
Wage costs	15	13	14	24	–	14*
Shortage of demand	26	22	24	24	25	24
Industrial disputes	–	3	1	–	–	–
Other problems	18	28	21	17	20	18
Base (= 100%)	46	34	80	25	17	42

Source: 1985 and 1988 OSG Surveys
* significant at the 5 per cent level

Table 6.8 Annual turnover in 1984 by gender of owner/manager – retail, catering and other services

	All firms			Sole owners only		
	Male	Female	All	Male	Female	All
	(column percentages)					
Less than £17,000	20	32	25	21	36	27
£17,000 to £49,999	20	32	25	26	36	30
£50,000 to £99,999	34	14	26	37	18	30
£100,000 to £249,999	20	14	18	11	9	10
Over £250,000	6	9	7	5	–	3
Base (= 100%)	35	22	57	19	11	30

Source: 1985 and 1988 OSG Surveys

estimating from our evidence the number of women (and men) who failed to set up in business due to lack of clearing bank finance.

Respondents were asked to say whether they experienced a range of problems within the first year of operation, and the results are summarized in Table 6.7. This table indicates that, in general, women founders were no more or less likely than men to suffer from problems during the vulnerable early years. The only significant difference appears in wage cost problems, which male sole owners were significantly more likely to suffer than their female counterparts. In addition, women were more likely than men to mention problems

Table 6.9 Profitability in 1985 by gender of owner/manager – retail, catering and other services

	All firms			Sole owners only		
	Male	Female	All	Male	Female	All
			(column percentages)			
Loss	13	20	16	14	22	18
Profit: 0–4.9%	27	26	27	32	11	23
Profit: 5–9.9%	10	31	19	5	33	18
Profit: 10% +	50	23	39	50	33	43
Base (= 100%)	48	35	83	22	18	40

Source: 1985 and 1988 OSG Surveys

Table 6.10 Number of employees (including owner) by gender of owner/manager – retail, catering and other services

	All firms			Sole owners only		
	Male	Female	All	Male	Female	All
			(column percentages)			
1–4	66	66	66	68	73	70
5–10	22	30	26	24	27	25
11–14	9	2	6	3	–	2
25+	3	2	2	5	–	3
Base (= 100%)	77	56	133	38	36	64

Source: 1985 and 1988 OSG Surveys

other than the ones specified by the interviewer. The further problems mentioned covered a variety of issues such as VAT and problems with particular customers, but there appear to be no major differences between the type of problems mentioned by male founders and those mentioned by females.

CHARACTERISTICS OF BUSINESSES IN 1985

The evidence on the characteristics of the businesses run by men and women in 1985 in terms of turnover, profitability and employment are now considered.

Table 6.8 shows that female-owned businesses were concentrated at the lower levels of turnover, with almost two-thirds having an annual turnover in 1984 of less than £50,000, compared with a figure of 40 per

Table 6.11 Composition of workforce in 1985 by gender of owner/manager – retail, catering and other services

		All firms			Sole owners only		
		Male	Female	All	Male	Female	All
Males	No.	214	41	255	112	6	118
	% of total	47	16	36	45	7	36
of which:							
Full-time	No.	148	31	179	61	2	63
	% of total	32	12	25	25	2	19
Part-time	No.	66	10	76	51	4	55
	% of total	14	4	11	21	5	17
Females	No.	244	210	454	135	78	213
	% of total	53	84	64	55	93	64
of which:							
Full-time	No.	83	104	187	24	45	69
	% of total	18	41	26	10	54	21
Part-time	No.	161	106	267	111	33	144
	% of total	35	42	38	45	39	44
Total workforce		458	251	709	247	84	331

Source: 1985 and 1988 OSG Surveys

cent for male-owned businesses. However, there is no significant difference in the mean levels of turnover of male- and female-owned businesses, with the average figure being around £75,000 for both groups. Male-owned businesses tend to be more profitable than those owned and managed by women, although this difference is less marked amongst sole owners (see Table 6.9). It is not clear whether this reflects an inherently better performance by male managers or a weaker profit orientation on the part of women entrepreneurs. Both interpretations are possible on the statistical evidence, and research of a different order is required before either can be substantiated.

Female-owned businesses are smaller than average in terms of the number of people employed. Women entrepreneurs in the retail, catering and service sectors employed an average of 4.4 workers (including themselves) compared with an average size of male-owned businesses of 5.9 workers. This difference is not statistically significant. Table 6.11 presents interesting evidence that women business owners are more likely to employ other women than are male entrepreneurs. Only 16 per cent of the people employed by female-run businesses were men, as compared with 47 per cent in the male-owned

A comparative study 81

Table 6.12 Change in volume of turnover 1982–4 by gender of owner/manager – retail, catering and other services

	All firms			Sole owners only		
	Male	Female	All	Male	Female	All
	(column percentages)					
Increased	66	52	60	66	44	56
Remained static	20	32	25	17	35	25
Decreased	15	16	15	17	22	19
Base (= 100%)	61	44	105	29	23	52

Source: 1985 and 1988 OSG Surveys

Table 6.13 Introduction of new technology 1982–5 by gender of owner/manager – retail, catering and other services

	All firms			Sole owners only		
	Male	Female	All	Male	Female	All
	(column percentages)					
Office functions	15	18	16	8	25	14
Production processes	31	23	27	31	30	31
Components	23	6	17	23	–	11
Storage etc.	18	13	17	19	–	14

Source: 1985 and 1988 OSG Surveys

businesses. It also appears that women business owners are more likely than their male counterparts to employ females on a full-time rather than a part-time basis. These differences in employment structure are clearly explained to some degree by the propensity of women to start up businesses in areas within the sectors under consideration such as hairdressing and retailing ladies' clothing in which women employees are traditionally more numerous. However, it may well be the case that women business owners tend to have a preference for female rather than male employees, a point which emerged in the study by Carter and Cannon (1988a).

Tables 6.12, 6.13 and 6.14 provide some indicators of the performance of the surveyed firms from 1982 to 1984/5. These tables reveal no significant differences over this period between the performances of male- and female-owned businesses. Women, particu-

82 Women in business

Table 6.14 Employment change 1982-5 by gender of owner/manager – retail, catering and other services

	All firms			Sole owners only		
	Male	Female	All	Male	Female	All
Total employment in 1982	297	144	441	142	51	193
Total employment in 1985	350	167	517	187	57	244
Percentage change 1982–85	17.8	16.0	17.2	31.7	11.8	26.4
No. of firms	59	37	96	28	17	45

Source: 1985 and 1988 OSG Surveys

Table 6.15 Position of firm in 1988 by gender of owner/manager – retail, catering and other services

	All firms			Sole owners only		
	Male	Female	All	Male	Female	All
	(column percentages)					
Still in existence	74	70	72	74	58	67
Known to have ceased trading	14	4	10	13	4	9
Not traced	12	27	18	13	39	23
Base (= 100%)	77	56	133	38	26	64

Source: 1985 and 1988 OSG Surveys

larly sole owners, were slightly less likely than men to have experienced growth in the volume of turnover between 1982 and 1984, and slightly more likely to have experienced no change in turnover levels. There appear to be no major differences between men and women owners in respect of their propensity to introduce new technology (Table 6.13), and Table 6.14 indicates that employment growth amongst female-owned businesses was approximately the same in percentage terms as that of businesses owned by men. However, when sole owners are separated out in the analysis, a faster employment growth rate is indicated amongst male-owned businesses.

CHANGES BETWEEN 1985 AND 1988

In the 1988 follow-up survey, 127 of the 226 firms covered in the foregoing analysis were re-interviewed, of which forty were owned and

Table 6.16 Changes in turnover and profitability 1984–5 by gender of owner/manager – retail, catering and other services

	All firms			Sole owners only		
	Male	Female	All	Male	Female	All
	(column percentages)					
Turnover						
Increased	58	55	57	62	46	56
Remained static	21	32	26	19	39	27
Decreased	21	13	17	19	15	18
Profitability						
Increased	51	51	51	57	46	53
Remained static	26	32	29	19	39	27
Decreased	23	16	20	24	15	21
Base (= 100%)	39	31	70	21	13	34

Source: 1985 and 1988 OSG Surveys

managed by women. Table 6.15 summarizes the position in 1988 of the original 133 firms which were in the retailing, catering and other services sectors. Ninety-six of these firms were known to be still trading at the end of 1988, of which seventy-eight responded to the follow-up survey. Thirteen firms are known to have ceased trading by 1988, and a further twenty-four could not be traced. It cannot be assumed that all of the last group of firms had, in fact, ceased trading, but it would not be unreasonable to conclude that this was the case for the majority of them.[2] No significant differences between male- and female-owned businesses were reached in terms of overall 'survival rates', although women-owned businesses, particularly those with women as sole owners, proved more difficult to trace than those run by men.

The turnover and profitability performances of women-owned businesses were more stable than those of male-owned firms, as is evident in Table 6.16. Thirty-two per cent of women reported no changes in the turnover and/or profitability of their businesses, compared with 21 and 26 per cent of men. In terms of the numbers employed there are differences between the firms owned by men and women. Employment in male-owned businesses declined at a marginally more rapid rate than employment in female-owned businesses. Women sole owners showed a small increase. In addition, women had tended to create more jobs in their businesses than they had predicted in 1985, whereas for men the opposite was the case (see Table 6.17).

Women in business

Table 6.17 Employment change 1985–7 by gender of owner/manager – retail, catering and other services

	All firms			Sole owners only		
	Male	Female	All	Male	Female	All
All firms						
Number of firms	39	36	75	21	13	34
Total employment in 1985	259	198	457	165	55	220
Total employment in 1987	232	187	419	145	57	202
Percentage change 1985–87	–10.4	–5.6	–8.3	–12.1	3.6	–8.2
Firms which gave a prediction in 1985						
Number of firms	23	24	47	12	10	22
Total employment in 1985	166	102	168	121	41	162
Expected employment in 1987	183	105	288	127	49	176
Actual employment in 1987	153	119	272	103	50	153

Source: 1985 and 1988 OSG Surveys

CONCLUSIONS

This chapter has illustrated that the differences between businesses run by men and women are fairly marginal in most respects, with very few differences being significant in statistical terms. However, it does appear to be the case that women founders of businesses are on average older than their male counterparts, are less well qualified, and that female founders are less likely than men to obtain start-up finance from commercial banks. The businesses run by women are smaller on average, in terms of the numbers employed but not in terms of financial turnover, and are less profitable than male-run businesses. Women entrepreneurs are much more likely than men to employ other women in their businesses. There are no major differences in the performance over time of male- and female-run businesses, although there is a slight tendency for businesses run by women to remain more stable in terms of turnover and profits and to increase employment.

These conclusions do not, however, throw a great deal of light on the hypothesis that many women are deterred from setting up businesses due to real or perceived discrimination on the part of financiers and/or potential clients. In order to investigate this issue fully it would be necessary to identify and interview women and men who had attempted but failed to set up in business. Our study has indicated, however, that the characteristics and performance of those women who do manage to set up and remain in business do not appear

A comparative study 85

to differ markedly from those of male entrepreneurs and their businesses.

NOTES

1 The 1985 survey was sponsored by the Occupations Study Group (OSG) and the 1988 survey by the Department of Employment. The authors would like to express their gratitude for this funding, but it should be emphasized that the sponsors bear no responsibility for any views expressed in this chapter. A more detailed description of the 1985 OSG survey can be found in Rajan and Pearson (1986).
2 Data on the registration and deregistration of firms for VAT (Ganguly 1985) would suggest an annual failure rate of around 9 per cent, which would translate into 67 of the surveyed firms.

7 Business start-up training
The gender dimension

Patricia Richardson and Christina Hartshorn

This chapter looks at two examples of business start-up training which have specifically targeted women, both younger women entering the labour market for the first time and older women who are either unemployed or returning to the labour market after raising a family. It is argued that women face a double disadvantage in trying to start up and run their own business. First, women have not traditionally been seen as business owners, and are under-represented in the small business sector. Second, women perform a dual role in that they are almost always responsible for domestic and family concerns whether they are economically active or not (see Epstein this volume). The chapter discusses the training programmes that the authors have developed, which in their style, content and timing set out to meet the special needs of women contemplating self-employment.[1]

THE ENTERPRISE CLIMATE

Since the late 1970s, governments have encouraged small business start-ups and the promotion of self-employment as an 'employment' option. This has been done both directly through the provision of finance, advice services, and training schemes and indirectly through changes in Government policy and legislation affecting the small business sector. As early as 1983 the Department of Industry could state that in the previous four years no less than ninety-eight measures had been specifically introduced to benefit small firms (Curran 1986). Since then many more initiatives have emerged, providing a complex network of support to small and medium enterprises (SME sector) (see, for example, Government White Paper 1986; *Employment Gazette* 1988a and Department of Employment 1989). What has been the rationale behind this promotion of small enterprise development? The reasons given for this advocacy have been wide-ranging – from wealth creation and stimulating economic growth, to encouraging the 'self-made person' ethic. Increasingly throughout the 1980s, however, the promotion of self-employment and business start-up was linked to unemployment and seen as an important tool for reducing the large numbers of unemployed found throughout the UK.

This objective was clearly set out in a Government White Paper which said, 'The prime aim of the Department of Employment is to encourage the development of an enterprise economy. The way to reduce unemployment is through more businesses, more self employment and greater wealth creation all leading to more jobs'(*Government White Paper* 1986, inside cover; see also *Employment Gazette* 1988b).

The Government has demonstrated this belief by supporting specific enterprise initiatives for the unemployed, such as the Enterprise Allowance Scheme (EAS) and Enterprise Training within Employment Training. They have also supported initiatives aimed at promoting and developing an 'enterprise culture' in Britain from mini enterprise projects and Technical and Vocational Education Initiatives (TVEI) in schools through to Enterprise in Higher Education in Universities and Colleges. Whilst the Government has carried out an 'enterprise awareness' campaign aimed at the public in general there has also been a large number of measures specifically targeted on those areas and people most affected by unemployment. These also tend to be those areas and groups which have had no tradition of self-employment or small business ownership. For example, measures have been targeted on older industrial areas, such as South Wales, the North of England, and many parts of Scotland, where there has been a long tradition of local people working in large organizations, so generating a strong employee culture. This targeted approach is amply illustrated by the initiatives of British Coal, British Steel, and British Shipbuilders in these areas.

Similarly, measures have been aimed at groups particularly susceptible to unemployment, such as young people, those from ethnic minority backgrounds, and those with disabilities. For example, the Prince's Youth Business Trust, Livewire, and Instant Muscle have all concentrated their efforts on helping young people under the age of 25 to start up in business.

One group which has been classified as both disadvantaged and non-traditional entrepreneurs has not, until very recently, been specifically singled out for assistance – they are women. Unlike other disadvantaged groups there have been few targeted measures to assist women enter self-employment or business ownership. Indeed, some initiatives such as the Enterprise Allowance Scheme effectively dis-

88 Women in business

Table 7.1 Percentage increase in self-employed by sex 1979–88 – Great Britain

	All self-employed	Self-employed with employees	Self-employed without employees
Men	65.6	29.9	91.3
Women	137.1	87.8	166.9
All persons	79.1	39.9	106.4

Source: Department of Employment 1989: 27

Table 7.2 Self-employment by sex, 1979–88 – United Kingdom

	Numbers of self-employed (thousand)			As a percentage of workforce in employment		
	Male	Female	Total	Male	Female	Total
December 1979	1,586	374	1,960	10.3	3.7	7.7
December 1980	1,659	408	2,067	11.1	4.1	8.3
December 1981	1,697	448	2,145	11.8	4.6	8.9
December 1982	1,703	493	2,196	12.1	5.1	9.3
December 1983	1,804	554	2,359	12.8	5.6	9.8
December 1984	1,939	614	2,554	13.6	6.1	10.4
December 1985	1,982	636	2,619	13.9	6.2	10.7
December 1986	2,071	673	2,743	14.6	6.4	11.1
December 1987	2,204	719	2,923	15.1	6.5	11.4
December 1988	2,297	750	3,048	15.5	6.6	11.7

Source: Department of Employment 1989: 25

criminate against considerable numbers of women.[2] One possible reason for this lack of targeting is the fact that official unemployment statistics in Britain have consistently undercounted the numbers of women looking for work (Martin and Roberts 1984; Allen 1989; Allen and Truman 1992). Because few women appear as officially unemployed, there has been little need to remove them from the register and thus less impetus to target measures on helping them start up in business.

WOMEN IN BUSINESS

Despite a lack of specific assistance to date, the number of women entering self-employment and small business ownership is increasing. As Table 7.1 shows, between 1979 and 1988 female self-employment

Table 7.3 Female self-employment as a percentage of total self-employment – regional analysis 1989

Region	Percentage	Region	Percentage
Scotland	20.3	Wales	26.0
North	25.8	North-West	26.0
Yorkshire and Humberside	25.4	East Midlands	24.0
West Midlands	27.0	South-West	26.5
East Anglia	27.0	South-East	23.8

Source: Employment Gazette 1989

increased by 137 per cent as compared to an increase of only 66 per cent for males. As can be seen in Table 7.2, the number of self-employed women doubled over the same period, although this represents only one-third of the number of self-employed men. Similarly, in 1982 only 10 per cent of participants on the government's Enterprise Allowance Scheme were women, but by 1988 this figure had increased to 32 per cent. Out of a total of 101,360 people on the scheme in 1988, there were 32,112 women (Skinner 1989). This increase follows similar start-up patterns elsewhere in the world (see Hisrich and Brush 1983 with respect to the United States, and Halpern and Szurek 1989 for some comparative statistics on Europe).

Having noted this increase in women's business ownership, nevertheless by 1989 women still formed less than 30 per cent of all business owners in the UK. Table 7.3 illustrates the regional variations within this figure.

To answer the question of why more women are setting up their own businesses, a number of factors need to be explored. No single factor motivates women to start up in business. Women, just as much as men, are found to be motivated by a wide range of factors and circumstances in their lives (Broadley 1990). For example, both women and men have turned to starting their own business as a direct response to unemployment. The numbers of women who have received support from the EAS reflect this.

Also, the general awareness campaign run by the Government to inculcate a sense of the enterprise culture reaches women as well as men, and women are made more aware of enterprise as an option. This is particularly so for women who are re-entering the economy after an absence and who discover that their original or current skills are redundant. Such women are more likely to be reviewing the various options open to them in their transition back to paid work. One option is self-employment. Carter and Cannon (1988b) in their study of seventy women owner-managers identified a group they termed 'returners' who had been motivated to start up in business by the desire to return to economic activity on favourable terms (see also Halpern and Szurek 1989).

There are, however, certain factors and circumstances which are women-specific and result in 'gender' related motivations for start-up. For example, current demographic changes have led to a shortage of skilled labour in the economy, the much quoted 'demographic time bomb'. This has meant that women are seen as a key skills source and are being actively encouraged to return to the labour market. It is likely that such women returners will provide an increasingly fruitful source of female business owners.

In addition, the tradition of women seeking part-time work to augment the family income at no detriment to their home making role has been encouraged by the relaxation of laws relating to part-time work so that employers find it financially beneficial to employ part-timers.[3] Increasingly, however, women have been required to earn more, either because they are single parents or because they need to make a significant contribution to the family income. For these women, part-time work on low wages with minimum job security or protection offers few rewards. In this context starting a business is seen as an alternative where 'there is little to lose'. For example Holmquist and Sundin's (1989) study of 64,420 female entrepreneurs in Sweden found the main motivation for the women was to create something which would allow them the freedom to combine responsibility for the family with a fair income. Goffee and Scase (1987) identify this group as 'conventional' female entrepreneurs, motivated by a need for autonomy, to acquire their own money, but only in a way that is compatible with their domestic role.

For women who are underemployed, with little job satisfaction, self-employment is seen as a means of creating stimulating work over which they have a greater measure of control. This control extends beyond the workplace, enabling women to harmonize economic activity within a valued family environment.

The frustrations of the 'glass ceiling effect' (Hymounts 1986) has also motivated women to look towards business creation. Women often reach an invisible but unyielding promotional barrier within the managerial hierarchy of larger organizations, and self-employment is seen as a vehicle through which their personal needs can be satisfied. Carter and Cannon (1988a) identified such a group of 'high achievers', describing them as older women who had had successful careers and desired independence because of gender related career blocks or the desire for the flexibility to have a family which was not possible while in formal employment.

SUPPORT FOR SMALL BUSINESS START-UP

As mentioned earlier, there is a considerable range of help on offer to potential business owners. These initiatives are wide-ranging both in their scope and format, and in the type of organizations which deliver them. Table 7.4 shows a simple categorization of providers and the 'enabling mechanisms' provided.

Some of those starting up in business do not need or wish to use any of the assistance available. They have, or think they have, the skills, knowledge and resources to start a business and go ahead. Others will need and use some, if not all, aspects of the assistance available. It is presumed that those groups who are 'non-traditional' entrepreneurs rely heavily on all of these enabling mechanisms to help them start-up in business. Women are one of these groups.

Perhaps the most important enabling mechanism for 'non-traditional' entrepreneurs is training. It is through training that people are able to develop business skills and knowledge so that they know how to start up and manage their own business. Counselling and advice are important but they are best used for solving immediate problems. It does not necessarily impart skills to clients and therefore enable them to tackle problems themselves. Indeed, one-to-one counselling can generate problems of dependency if clients become reliant on business counsellors to solve their problems.

Training is used for developing the person, their ideas, and skills. The single most important resource of any small business is the owner-manager, and training that person, it could be argued, is the greatest investment in the business and has the greatest impact.

WOMEN'S BUSINESS START-UP TRAINING IN SCOTLAND

In 1986 the Women's Enterprise Unit was initiated by the Scottish Enterprise Foundation (SEF) at the University of Stirling, to effect a positive policy of encouraging and enabling more women to take up business ownership. At the same time a local Enterprise Trust, Bathgate Area Support for Enterprise (BASE) Ltd, in West Lothian, had identified a gap in their services.[4] By mid 1987 both organizations had independently decided to provide enterprise training programmes specifically for women.[5] SEF's first Enterprise Training for Women business programme started in September 1987 and provided training

Table 7.4 Some examples of the assistance available for business start-up*

Providers	Advice and support	Enabling mechanisms Training and education	Finance and resources
Central Government (including Training Agency)	• Small Firms Service • SDA Business Counsellors • Euro Information Centre • In Glasgow Programme	• SDA Marketing Courses • Employment Training (Enterprise) • Graduate Enterprise • British Steel loans	• Enterprise Allowance Scheme • Business Expansion Scheme • The Enterprise Initiative • British Coal Enterprise loans
Local Government	• Economic Development Units • Innovation Centres, eg Strathclyde • Co-operative and Community Business Development Agencies	• FE Colleges, business courses, e.g. accounting, marketing, management, etc. • Local authority training programmes	• Empresarial Initiative in Strathclyde • Enterprise Boards – loan funds • Loan and grant schemes, e.g. SEEDCO and SWIBS • Stirling District Council
Private sector	• Livewire (Shell) • Secondees to Enterprise Agencies/Trusts • Banks – advice and literature • Accountants	• BP Bright Ideas Project • Sponsored Exhibitions and Conferences • STEP (Shell) • Women in Business	• Livewire • PYSBT Fund • Bank loans
Joint public and private organizations	• Enterprise Agency/Trust • Counselling • Business clubs	• Enterprise Trust/Agency • Start-up courses • WEDA network	• Loans and grants, e.g. Bathgate • Investment Fund
Others (including voluntary groups, EEC, etc.)	• Instant Muscle Counsellors • Project Fullemploy Counsellors • IRIS Network	• URBED courses • Women in Enterprise • ESF courses for start-ups • Co-operative training, e.g. ICOM	• Local Employment Initiatives (EEC Grants)

*At the time of writing, responsibility for much of the training support given to business start-ups is being transferred to the Training Enterprise Councils in England and Wales, and the Local Enterprise Councils in Scotland.

for any unemployed women who wanted to start-up in business and also for six women who wanted to become business advisers. BASE's first Women's Enterprise Programme was launched in October 1987 and catered for women over 25 years of age who wanted to start up in business. To date both SEF and BASE have each provided six gender-specific enterprise training programmes.[6] In providing such training both organizations recognized the different experiences and needs of women. Currently most business start-up programmes are for both men and women. In general, the materials used on these programmes and the orientation of the training is geared towards men and their experiences. Women experience socialization, education and work differently from men (Goldstein 1984; Northern Ireland EOC 1987 and Vokins this volume). Recognition of this has led, historically, to the provision of gender-specific training in other economic sectors. For example in strategic terms women were (and still are) perceived as being under-represented in the science and engineering sectors, therefore a national set of positive strategies for recruitment and training, Women into Science and Engineering (WISE), was agreed. A more specific example is the SCOTEC Technician Certificate in Electrical and Electronic Engineering which Stevenson College, Edinburgh first provided in 1985. Existing training courses had had extremely low numbers of women participants and the sector needed more qualified test and control engineers, so a gender-specific course was designed. What this recognized was the previous experience of the women and the expectations of a gendered culture to which they belonged. Whilst the course was for women only, participants were required to achieve the level of skill demanded by national criteria.

It is important to build on the experience of such examples of positive action as a model for this kind of approach to business start-up training. Women in general have less formal work experience, and fewer business and managerial skills than men, and tend to bear the prime responsibility for family affairs. Furthermore, for some women a business training programme will be their first taste of education for some years. For many women their very different experience and skill base frequently results in a lack of self-confidence and in turn this prevents them from utilizing the start-up assistance that is available. These different needs of women are discussed below with respect to business training, under the four headings of content, time, process, and support. We feel these four elements of a training programme are the most important factors to be taken into account when developing specific business start-up training courses for women.

CONTENT

The content of women's business start-up programmes needs to be different from those of men. We are not talking about a 'softer option', a term sometimes applied to women-only training courses. What we are saying is that women are looking at the self-employment option from a different perspective to men. Business start-up skills, management skills, and personal skills must be fundamental to any first stage enterprise course. Our programmes for women also teach and encourage personal development. Broadley (1990), in his review of barriers to start-up for women going into business found that a number of studies highlighted a lack of self-confidence as a major barrier (Andersen 1989; Lawrence 1989; McColl 1989). A loss of confidence is experienced particularly by women returners and is associated with their length of time out of the labour market. This factor is compounded by societal expectations that women should perform a dual role (Barron and Norris 1976). Whether a woman is economically active or not, she is almost always responsible for domestic and family concerns (Oakley 1982). Personal development seeks to increase confidence and encourage women to explore roles as entrepreneurs. The use of case studies and assertiveness training on our programmes enables women to 'test out' future situations which threaten to produce potential role conflict. This need for 'affective socialization' has been recognized as a critical, but all too often absent, element of small business education (Curran and Stanworth 1989: 15).

Personal development not only helps to give women confidence but also aims to help women take control and manage their own lives (Davidson and Cooper 1983). It also places a strong emphasis on valuing previous work and non-work experiences, and learning to transfer the skills acquired through them. The experience, for instance, of bringing up a family as a single parent and/or on a low income means that many women are very good at financial and time management, although they do not recognize these skills or associate them with the business 'labels' applied to them.

TIME

The time element needs to be considered in two respects. First, the duration of the training programmes and second, when and at what time they take place.

Duration

Throughout the last five years business start-up programmes appear to have shrunk progressively, from the three-month Start Your Own Business courses, to the two-day Mini-Business Enterprise Programmes. It is questionable whether what has been termed a 'microwave' approach to business training will be able to provide the appropriate quality of training needed to help people start up in business: 'the length of small business educational programmes on offer, seems absurd, when set against the knowledge and complexities of the multifunctional task of successfully operating a small business' (Curran and Stanworth 1989: 15). Short training programmes are particularly at odds with the requirements for compensatory learning and experience needed by women. The SEF and BASE programmes run for at least ten weeks and there is considerable scope for extending the period of enterprise training given under Employment Training (ET). The duration is important for five reasons in particular.

First, many women, in particular returners, have not been in a formal work environment for a number of years. Consequently they lack or have a less developed network of potential business contacts than many men. They do not have the 'old boy network' to call upon for advice and guidance. Studies such as Hisrich and Brush (1983) in the USA and Carter and Cannon (1988a) in Britain have highlighted the fact that because of their lack of management experience women are often deprived of useful business networks, which can put them at a disadvantage in highly competitive markets. Training programmes using specialists from the private sector and existing business owners as speakers provide women participants with the opportunities and time to begin to develop their own networks.

Second, women by and large lack the managerial, organizational, and financial skills needed to start up and run a business (Carter and Cannon 1988a; Andersen 1989). Longer training programmes enable women to learn and develop these skills gradually. Many women's domestic skills, such as people and time management, and household budgeting, are directly transferable to the business context. During the early stages of our programme we demonstrate that these 'domestic' skills present a strong foundation for learning what are more traditionally labelled business skills. This foundation is built on throughout the rest of the programme, with further business management and financial skills inputs.

Third, women tend not to have access to their own money or to any collateral for borrowing (Cannon et al. 1988). This applies particularly to women returners, although even if a woman has recently been in paid employment it is likely that she will have been earning considerably less than her male counterpart. She is likely therefore to have less collateral and a more limited credit history. Consequently, whatever their employment position prior to business start-up, women have to prepare extremely well to persuade others to support their business propositions financially (see Koper this volume). Women are further back along the track than men when starting in business and need to put themselves on an equal footing. A longer training programme gives women the time to assess their financial and other business needs, and to develop a strategy for meeting them.

Fourth, time is important because it provides space. Our programmes are taking women out of their home environment. For returners, home and community have been their known environment for several years. The programme gives them the opportunity to think about alternatives without the demands of children, family, and friends. Therefore, the time spent on the programme is useful not just for learning skills, but also in providing space for reassessing existing obligations and the new ones a business will produce.

Fifth, time is essential to operate and develop an active rather than a passive *style* of learning. This is discussed below under process.

When

The precise time that a programme is offered is very important. Many women are responsible for the care of dependants, be they children or older relatives. The timing of the programme schedule must take account of the responsibilities participants may have. The time at which a programme can be offered will also be determined by the source of funding, where it is physically located, and the area from which participants are drawn. Courses can be full-time, part-time, day or evening, and at different times of the year. Each of these may facilitate different groups of women.

Some programmes for women at SEF, for example, have been nationally based, attracting participants from throughout Scotland. They have been provided on a full-time basis, initially for five days a week, and later for three days a week. The women were paid allowances in order to reside locally for the days on which the programme is held. At Bathgate, courses have been provided on a part-time basis for three days a week from 9.30 a.m. to the early afternoon. All the women participants on such courses live locally and the hours are designed to accommodate school hours. In addition, both programmes offer financial assistance towards childcare whilst the women are on the programme.

PROCESS

It can be seen that the shorter the start-up programme, the greater the emphasis on content and the diminution of emphasis on process. A major barrier to a flexible learning process is the time constraint (Sym and Lewis 1987).

The processes used in our programmes are twofold. First there is an emphasis on active learning, and second an approach which is thematic and developmental. Business ownership is an isolating experience. There is not a team of valued colleagues with expertise to share. Active learning is used as a method of showing women how to manage their own learning. Women returners have been away from formal learning for some time and have often had negative educational experiences (see Jones this volume). It is therefore doubtful whether past learning experiences will be of use to them now as potential business start-ups or indeed in the future as business owners. Active learning encourages trainees to identify their own learning needs from objectives that they have set. They then write their own learning agenda and work towards fulfilling those objectives. This learning process transfers to the world of proprietorship, where problem solving and information management is central to maintenance and growth.

Active learning is a more appropriate method for skilling trainees where the content is skill rather than facts. The process ought to be active rather than passive 'talk and chalk', the aim being to give trainees control over the learning process. For example, the topic of market research is introduced experientially. Women participants are set a market research task to assess, for instance whether an on-campus hair salon would make enough money to live on. They later make a presentation of their findings to the class. They have thus learned *about* market research from 'doing'. Learning points are drawn from the experience by the tutor and reflected back to the women. They are then able to begin to undertake the market research necessary for their own particular business.

The thematic approach is exemplified by the marketing element of the programme. Each week a new marketing topic is covered. Thus rather than presenting marketing as a module, it is unfolded and developed so that by the end of the programme the women will have written the marketing section of their business plans. Lectures are used to transmit information and theoretical frameworks. Action learning workshops are then held, where each participant's particular business ideas and marketing plans are used as examples.

Process is integral to the concept of training for women, and is a feature of lengthy training. The more time available for training, the more balanced content and process can become. The shorter the time, the less process can be incorporated into the course.

SUPPORT

Another positive issue is that of support and encouragement, throughout and after the training programme. We have shown how women are supported both by the attention paid to course content and by the way the content is delivered. It is also important to have intra-group support as part of the learning process. The participants use each other as a resource, pooling knowledge, experience, and skills to develop their business. They learn to value what they know, and, by extension, themselves.

This mutual support process should also be used to form a network after the formal programme ends. This is particularly important when women are going to become sole traders, frequently working from home. This is a very isolating position. Research has shown that women can expect very little practical support from their family, be it help with domestic duties or activities directly related to the business. Goffee and Scase (1987) comment that while male business owners can expect a great deal of domestic and business support from their wives as a 'crucial source of unpaid labour', it is very rare for female entrepreneurs to receive the same assistance. A 1990 review of Scottish women starting up in business found that 'few of the women thought that they received much support with their businesses [and] even fewer felt that their family or friends were actively supportive with household duties' (Broadley 1990: 29; see also Andersen 1989). Women should therefore be encouraged to support each other after a training programme ends.

Indeed at Bathgate participants from the first two programmes continue to meet as a group on a regular basis and suggestions have been put forward to transform these meetings into a Women's Business Club. Women from a recent SEF programme have taken a further step and actually set up their own local business club entitled IBIS.

Women from the programmes trade with each other, and at Stirling two women from different programmes have subsequently formed a partnership. Providers at SEF and BASE have tried to encourage the support process further by teaming up with another Scottish training provider, Strathkelvin Enterprise Trust, to run a tripartite women's start-up programme. This involved running programmes in the three different locations but bringing the three groups together for some joint training days. This provided women participants with the opportunity to extend their contacts beyond their local network.

CONCLUSIONS AND THE WAY FORWARD

For the reasons given above we would argue that women's business training is and needs to be differentiated from that generally provided. It is not a matter of providing the same type of business course to women-only groups. Women have very different needs and require a different learning environment from that provided in mixed gender programmes. It is essential to incorporate the specific needs of women into programmes if we are to promote good and relevant training practice.

However, training cannot be isolated from the other mechanisms used to facilitate start-up. Training for women is a positive method to help them overcome the additional barriers they face as potential entrepreneurs. The way forward is for positive policies to be identified and implemented in the areas of advice, support, and financial assistance (Skinner 1989; see also Koper this volume).
training and a directory of good quality materials for such training.

However, training, cannot be isolated from the other mechanisms used to facilitate start-up. Training for women is a positive method to help them overcome the additional barriers they face as potential entrepreneurs. The way forward is for positive policies to be identified and implemented in the areas of advice, support, and financial assistance (Skinner 1989; see also Koper this volume).

At present the Advice and Support agencies have few women counsellors and most show little awareness of women's different needs (Chan 1988). Unless there is recognition from this sector, there is a danger that training for women will be seen as all that is required to enable more women to enter proprietorship. It is a relatively easy task to organize separate training, but it is much harder to counter the indifference shown by the other sectors of support (see Cannon et al. 1988, in particular on finance).

We have discussed two examples of business start-up training programmes specifically for women. There are others. In Scotland, for example, women's business programmes are run by Aberdeen Enterprise Trust, Workstart at Dundee, Paisley Enterprise Trust and Queen Margaret College in Edinburgh. However, it is very difficult to build up a picture of what is being provided where and by whom as there is no central collection or collation of initiatives directed at women, an issue raised in an EC study (Halpern and Szurek 1989). There is no national policy or strategy targeted at helping women through the process of business start-up. Moreover, we have no means of knowing how many and which women use Enterprise Agencies or other Advisory Services as there is a gender-blind approach to the collection of statistics (Chan 1988; Truman this volume).

Research needs to be carried out in all of these areas, and information gathered to build up a comprehensive picture of what type of help different agencies are providing to which groups of women. It is important to have this if we are to discover which forms of assistance are most effective and where the gaps in policy and provision exist. Only by doing this can a coherent strategy be developed with a comprehensive range of support mechanisms geared to helping more women survive in the establishment of business.

NOTES

1 This chapter does not set out to provide a comprehensive commentary on women in business. For example, the women who have participated in our programmes are predominantly white although they come from a very broad range of socio-economic backgrounds and have wide-ranging educational experiences – from those with no formal qualifications to those with higher degrees. The programmes have also catered primarily for traditional forms of ownership, though partnerships have been formed between course members during or after the programme.
2 Many women cannot qualify for the Enterprise Allowance Scheme because of the benefit eligibility rule. This determines that only those in direct receipt of benefit are eligible for support. Many women are in receipt of benefit through their male partners, who are taken to be the head of the household.
3 A proportion of the increase in the numbers of women who are self-employed is no doubt due to new employment practices. Women are being 'hired' on a self-employed basis rather than as casual labour or part-time employees (Hakim 1988).
4 BASE Ltd now operate as West Lothian Enterprise Ltd.
5 The earliest documented start-up courses which we have found are those which were held in Mid Wales (1984–85) by the Mid Wales Development Board and in Camden, London (1986–87) by Project Fullemploy (see Careers Research and Advisory Centre 1986). It was not until 1987 that enterprise training specifically for women took place in Scotland.
6 SEF has run the last two gender-specific programmes through Employment Training.

8 Not just for pin money
A case study of the West Midlands Clothing Business Start-Up Project

Davinder Kaur and Carol Hayden

INTRODUCTION

The workforce of the clothing industry in the West Midlands is predominantly female. Firms rely heavily on Asian women as factory machinists and homeworkers. As owners or managers of clothing businesses, however, women, and especially black women, are underrepresented.

The Clothing Business Start-Up Project was established to carry out training, advice, and support work aimed at maximizing the employment potential of new, small clothing businesses, particularly those run by women and black people within the inner city areas of the West Midlands. Initially the Project took the form of a year's pilot programme based at the West Midlands Clothing Resource Centre and was funded by the Barrow and Geraldine S. Cadbury Trust for a period of three years. The Project now forms a core part of the Clothing Resource Centre's work.

The Project started in response to an identified growth in the number of unemployed people trying to establish small make-through clothing businesses as co-operatives, sole traders, partnerships, etc. It had become clear that in addition to general business advice, such as is provided by a variety of agencies, many of the needs of the start-up business were quite specific to the clothing industry. Many general agencies themselves expressed concern that potential businesses were failing at an early stage due to lack of access to specialist advice. In addition, individuals trying to set up small clothing businesses had reported experiences of negative racial and gender stereotyping by both advisers and financiers as to the competence of women and black people to manage a business successfully.

The Project thus represents an innovative initiative in that it takes a sector-based and user friendly approach to the development of small business. The evaluation of the project (Kaur and Hayden 1990) was carried out both in terms of the benefits to the clothing businesses receiving support and in the wider context of sector based initiatives aimed at encouraging and sustaining self-employment among groups of people who have been at a disadvantage in the labour market.

BREAKING INTO THE CLOTHING BUSINESS

The West Midlands Clothing Resource Centre, established in 1986, was originally seen as working with existing, production line clothing manufacturers in the area to improve profitability and the working conditions of employees (see West Midlands Enterprise Board 1986, 1988; Hayden forthcoming). However, as the Centre started to become well known, it increasingly attracted a stream of enquiries about setting up small 'make through' clothing businesses. The majority of enquiries were from unemployed women who wanted, either individually or with one or two other partners, to try self-employment. Enquiries also started to arise from local business advice agencies who felt they needed specialist clothing-related advice to be of use to their pre-trading clients.

It was immediately clear that these potential clothing businesses had specific needs which had to be fulfilled in order to overcome the barriers that had already been experienced. These reflected both the characteristics of the individuals trying to start up businesses and the precise type of business they wished to establish. The people interested in setting up their own small 'make through' clothing businesses were typically young, black people, female or male with a design and/or craft training or older women with domestic sewing skills. These groups have traditionally worked in the clothing industry as relatively low-status employees rather than owner/managers (Phizacklea 1988).

Many women needing to contribute to the family income, or wanting financial independence, see self-employment as a meaningful and flexible way of using their skills. Self-employment may fit in better with domestic responsibilities and can offer more control and satisfaction than low paid, repetitive, part-time work which is often the only alternative (see Richardson and Hartshorn this volume). Women are therefore attracted to businesses which utilize their skills (many of which have been learnt in the context of domestic and voluntary work; for example, sewing, cleaning, cooking), and which draw on their existing social contacts and moreover can take place from a home base. For these reasons, clothing manufacture and clothing related businesses are very attractive to women. This does not, however, mean it is easier for women to start a clothing business, as the barriers to women's self-employment apply here as elsewhere.

The first barrier is that of finance. Women are often ineligible for various forms of financial assistance provided by the state. A major source of finance for unemployed people is the Enterprise Allowance Scheme (EAS). Fifty-six per cent of all clients seen in the Project were either already on EAS or were eligible for it. Eligibility criteria, however, include having been in receipt of unemployment benefit for at least six weeks before joining the scheme, and as many unemployed women are not in receipt of this benefit in their own right they do not qualify (see Richardson and Hartshorn this volume). There has been a widely voiced concern that the scheme discriminates against women. Twenty per cent of female project users were unemployed, but most were unlikely to be eligible for EAS to start their businesses. Obtaining loans from banks is also difficult if a woman has no property of her own to use as collateral. A widely expressed, albeit more subjective difficulty, is the discriminatory attitude which women experience from predominantly male bank managers who apparently have little 'confidence' in women running businesses. Many, and women in particular, complained to the Resource Centre about not being taken seriously by banks; their capability and credibility were questioned time and again (see Koper this volume). They were given the impression that they were thought to lack the motivation and ambition necessary to start a business and were doing so only for 'pin money'. In some cases where a loan was actually granted, women had to get their husband's formal agreement. In one case a woman was told by her bank manager that if all else failed (that is, if she were unable to raise finance for her business), she could always find herself a 'sugar daddy'.

The second problem faced by women is in the area of obtaining advice. Some of the growing number of 'enterprise agency' type organizations are very supportive. However, in many, women users perceived that the staff found it difficult to provide appropriate assistance to women wanting to set up in business. This is to some extent explained by women's self-employment being concentrated in certain occupations, such as clothing, of which male agency staff may have little experience. Research by Carter and Cannon (1988b) showed that for most female entrepreneurs there was a close link between their previous work and self-employment, or that self-employment was achieved by building the business from hobbies or unpaid domestic skills. The women also perceive the staff as not always understanding their

104 Women in business

Table 8.1 Clients by race and gender 1988-9

	Female No.	Male No.	Total No.
White	56	12	68
Afro-Caribbean	54	20	74
Asian	23	29	52
Total	133	61	194

domestic responsibilities and, therefore, neither their reasons for seeking to take up self-employment nor the form they wish the self-employment to take. Hakim (1989) found that the two most important reasons for women entering self-employment were independence and being able to choose when to work. This need for flexibility was not among men's important reasons. The realization of this need is apparent from the 1989 Labour Force Survey, which showed 46.5 per cent of women in self-employment working less than 30 hours, compared to 6.6 per cent of men (Department of Employment 1990).

Black people also experience considerable barriers to self-employment, although as discussed below in the context of Project users' experiences, the nature of these tend to vary between ethnic groups. Work done by the Centre for Research in Ethnic Relations at Warwick University and published by the West Midlands Low Pay Unit (Rice and Patel 1988) illustrated the concentration of black people in low paid, unskilled jobs. This disadvantage, combined with an unemployment rate of 22 per cent for ethnic minority groups in the West Midlands compared with 9 per cent for white people in the region, means that for many black people, as for women, self-employment may be the only viable alternative (Department of Employment 1990).

THE NEW CLOTHING ENTREPRENEURS

During the first year of the Project, between March 1988 and March 1989, 194 clients benefited from advice, support and/or training courses. Over two-thirds of these clients were female and nearly two-thirds were black. (Only 6 per cent of all clients were white men). These statistics, obtained from the monitoring systems used throughout the Project, support our original perception that most individuals who are attracted to small scale clothing manufacture are black and/or female. Table 8.1 shows the detailed breakdown of the Project's clients by race and gender.

Overall, the largest proportion of clients (38 per cent) are Afro-

Table 8.2 Initial employment status by race – female clients

Status	White	Afro-Caribbean	Asian	Total	%
Self-employed (in Business)	12	5	2	19	14
Employment (full-time)	6	7	2	15	11
Employment (part-time)	10	2	3	15	11
Unemployed	28	40	16	84	63
Total	56	54	23	133	100

Caribbean. Unlike the Asian population, this ethnic group has virtually no presence in the established 'production line' clothing industry. It is noticeable, however, that Afro-Caribbean women represent 41 per cent of all female clients, while Afro-Caribbean men comprise only 33 per cent of all male clients. In contrast, Asian men make up nearly half of all male clients while Asian women represent only 17 per cent of all female clients.

Most of the clients lived in inner city areas of the West Midlands County and we estimated that over three-quarters of the businesses would be owned by people from the inner city.

At the time of first approaching the Project, 61 per cent of all clients were unemployed, 16 per cent had recently started their business and 23 per cent were employed. The pattern of unemployment and employment varies both by race and gender, as is shown by Tables 8.2 and 8.3. Of white men and women, approximately 50 per cent were unemployed and the remainder of the women were likely to be in part-time employment. This confirms the perception that many women, due to their domestic commitments, see home-based self-employment as a positive alternative to the low paid, part-time work otherwise available. Over 70 per cent of Afro-Caribbean men and women, and Asian women, were unemployed. This confirms the lack of employment opportunities for black people and explains why many young Afro-Caribbean people are attracted to self-employment as an alternative to unemployment. Small scale clothing manufacture involves relatively low start-up costs, builds on a possible design or technical training and offers scope for creative work with some degree of personal control. This last characteristic is inevitably lacking in the low skilled, low paid employment in which black people are concentrated through discrimination both in training and recruitment.

Table 8.3 Initial employment status by race – male clients

Status	White	Afro-Caribbean	Asian	Total	%
Self-employed (in Business)	4	2	6	12	20
Employment (full-time)	2	3	8	13	21
Employment (part-time)	–	–	1	1	2
Unemployed	6	15	14	35	57
Total	12	20	29	61	100

Asian men, in contrast to the other black clients, were relatively less likely to be unemployed, with over 50 per cent either having started in business or being employed. While not ignoring the discrimination all Asian people face within the labour market, these figures would seem to confirm a commonly held view that Asian men often view self-employment as a positive alternative to employment and are more likely to receive financial and family support to pursue this path.

It should be emphasized that women from both Asian and Afro-Carribean communities probably face the most severe difficulties when trying to obtain business finance or advice, and face the possibility of a double discrimination shown in attitudes towards their capability of running a business. They are very unlikely to own any personal capital either to use directly as an investment in the business or as security for bank lending.

The type of small business which the individual or groups of women coming to the Project were interested in establishing usually operates on a 'make-through' rather than a production line basis, and targets a specialist market by providing garments with a high design and quality input. Such businesses therefore face different problems from even the smaller production line firms who typically operate in the 'cut, make and trim' sector, which although it produces low profits, also carries a low risk and does not need design, pattern cutting, costing, pricing, and marketing skills. In contrast, the small make-through businesses need very specific, clothing related skills, and technical advice which is lacking within most of the West Midlands clothing industry. Examples of these technical areas are marketing, machinery, fabric sourcing, and access to designers. Several potential businesses have failed at an early stage because of lack of access to advice on the issues of what 'market' to target, what garments to produce, how to cost and price them and through which type of outlet to sell them. Some groups of women bought fabric from retailers, which reduced their profit margin because they did not know about appropriate wholesalers.

Small make-through clothing businesses also experience specific market circumstances that are different from those which affect other small businesses. Clothing manufacture involves the production of 'Fast Moving Consumer Goods' (FMCG). Such markets are characterized by a high design content, reaction to changing consumer taste and a large number of sub-markets differentiated by quality, style, and price. Other similar FMCG markets include furniture, jewellery, and processed food. Manufacturing units producing for these markets tend to range considerably in size so that smaller units generally need to concentrate on high value production as they cannot produce the volume necessary to compete on the basis of price against the larger manufacturers.

Within many other sectors it is not so vital for small firms to find a specific, high value, market niche. Many service sectors are indeed made up predominantly of small firms such as those who carry out decorating, small scale construction, car repairs, cleaning, and so on, who operate at no cost disadvantage with their larger competitors. Moreover, these service firms, together with smaller manufacturing firms which produce non-consumer goods (e.g. suppliers of components and materials), tend not to experience the widely fluctuating style changes that the clothing industry faces. Firms in the FMCG markets are therefore continually keeping up with fashion which, as a concept, may involve numerous different looks or tastes at any one time, reflecting the diverse sub-markets.

Over 60 per cent of EAS survivors are concentrated into four main sectors – construction, retail, personal domestic services, and repairs to consumer goods and vehicles. If enterprise agencies' services reflect this distribution, it is not surprising that unemployed individuals wishing to enter clothing manufacture either alone or within a group tend to feel that general business advice and training does not cover, and indeed is sometimes irrelevant to, their particular enterprise and the market in which they operate. Unfortunately this is often not realized until the business has actually been embarked upon.

The National Audit Office's report on the Enterprise Allowance Scheme (Department of Employment 1988b) shows that an average of only 57 per cent of entrants were still trading three years later. Around 40 per cent of entrants drop out within the first year or eighteen months (i.e. after the weekly allowance is withdrawn). The Audit Office recommended that the survival rate could be improved not only

108 *Women in business*

by the use of viability tests but also by 'better business training'. It would seem reasonable that this could include sector specific issues facing new businesses.

OLD NEEDS – NEW AIMS

The sector based Business Start-Up Project was designed to help participants address general issues of whether they actually wanted to establish a clothing business (or, at an even broader level, to become self-employed), what sort of business they wanted to establish (manufacturing, retailing, design, type of garments), and the price range and how to appraise the likely viability of their business idea. The Project aimed to provide detailed specialist advice which was not available elsewhere. Much of this was related to marketing, technical or financial skills. Figure 8.1 shows examples of these specialist areas as originally perceived.

Taking acccount of characteristics, skills, and needs of the likely users and the range of business advice already available, the Business Start-Up Project therefore aimed to provide specialist advice and training for individuals establishing small, make-through clothing businesses.

Access to advice, training, and finance is of crucial importance when starting a business. Most of the clients were referred to the Project by an Enterprise Agency or a similar advisory organization (e.g. Project Full Employ, Co-operative Development Agency). The Project encourages this and liaises with such agencies. Clients were also referred to the Project via the respective Economic Development Units (EDUs) of local Councils with whom the Project works closely. Of the total number of clients approaching the Project, ninety-four people (48 per cent) were also attending a general business skills training course. A far lower number, twenty-four people (12 per cent), were attending a technical or craft skills course.

As shown by Table 8.4, women from all three groups as well as Afro-Caribbean men were more likely to be attending a business skills course than either white or Asian men. This probably reflects the fact that self-employment is a relatively new option for most women and for Afro-Caribbean men. White and Asian men, on the other hand, may feel they have 'picked up' much of the necessary information and business skills through family or personal experience of running a business. It may also be that white and Asian men experience fewer barriers to establishing businesses, particularly in terms of access to finance. This is likely to be so in terms of availability of personal and

The main needs which the project aimed to address were as follows:

Finance
Accessing finance and approaching banks – including ways of helping bank managers to understand clothing businesses and overcoming the problems of collateral for loan finance.
- Costing garments – how to cost garments and calculate profit margins.
- Business Planning – understanding the importance of a business plan.

Marketing
Sales and marketing – how to target a specialist market and conduct market research surveys
- How to sell and market a range of garments.
- How to prepare mail order catalogues and organize party-plans.
- Provision of names and addresses of buying offices of chain stores, department stores, and export buying houses.
- Trade journals – for information on future trends in styles, colours, shapes, designs, and fabrics.
- Exhibitions – information about exhibitions relevant to their business idea, dates, locations, and how to make contacts.

Technical information/production management
- Fabrics – names and addresses of wholesale suppliers, locally and nationally, and prices of fabrics. List of companies who would be willing to sell fabrics in small quantities.
- Sewing machines – names and addresses of suppliers. Information on different types of sewing machines, sewing threads, and needles; access to use of expensive industrial sewing machines.
- Trimmings – names and addresses of suppliers of trimmings, button, zips, laces etc.
- Patterns – where to get the patterns made from original designs or have the patterns graded into different sizes.
- Training courses – locally available skills related courses on pattern drafting and grading. Use of industrial sewing machines. Sewing skills training for 'make-through' production.

Network and resources
- Drop in/phone advice – to complement and follow on from structured training courses.
- Information and library resources – to provide regular details of new market developments, retailer contacts, training courses etc.
- Development of a network – to provide contact with other similar and related businesses (e.g. access to designers).

Figure 8.1 Needs of the trainees

family capital and by virtue of financial institutions having more positive perceptions of their ability to run a business.

For the Clothing Business Start-Up Project to fill the gap in existing

Table 8.4 Proportions of different client groups attending business skills courses[a]

	Female %	Male %	Total %	Nos
White	41	25	39	68
Afro-Caribbean	70	60	68	74
Asian	52	24	37	52
Total	54	36	48	
Nos (Total clients)	133	61	100	194

Note: [a]Each entry shows the proportion of *each* client group attending business skills courses. E.g. 41 per cent of white females, 60 per cent of Afro-Caribbean males, 48 per cent of all clients.

provision effectively it employed a suitable individual to organize and co-ordinate the planned training and support services. The Co-ordinator, Davinder Kaur, commenced work in October 1987. She had had eight years' experience in the clothing industry in the UK and Western Europe, including production, retail and wholesale management, marketing and buying for import/export. She also had experience in community work, particularly of working with Asian women. It was vital that the Project was based at the Clothing Resource Centre in order to provide specialist clothing services. The Project and the Co-ordinator had to show an understanding of the type of business in terms of the clothing industry and small business development. In addition, the Project Co-ordinator needed to be able to demonstrate a practical understanding of the economic and social problems experienced by the likely clients, of whom a high proportion were expected to be black women. Only by taking both these aspects into account would the Project provide a service more specialist than, and generally different from, that already provided by existing enterprise agencies.

The West Midlands Clothing Resource Centre based in Smethwick, Sandwell, was established as a subsidiary company of the West Midlands Enterprise Board, following the abolition of the West Midlands County Council in 1986. The Centre was set up to work with the local clothing industry with the aim of improving quality, efficiency and skills in the sector. This was seen as being necessary if the industry was to move away from low profit sub-contracting work into higher quality, high value production allowing opportunities for improvements in employees' pay and conditions to occur.

The Centre has a staff of six people and houses a computerized bureau operated by technical staff for the use of local firms. The computer bureau provides high technology pattern-drafting, lay-planning and design facilities. The Centre also gives advice and information on business grants, exporting and marketing, holds seminars and exhibitions, and runs training courses for mangagement and supervisory staff in the clothing industry. It undertakes consultancy on design projects, production, marketing and assessment of training needs for local companies. Firms and individuals have access to the Centre's library, which contains a wide range of technical information on the clothing industry and markets.

A HELPING HAND - SUPPORT AND TRAINING

The Start-Up Project supported new businesses by offering advice which ranged from very basic information, for example fabric sourcing, to more technical information such as specialized knitting or embroidery machines, or regulations regarding export of clothing to the EC, the USA and elsewhere. Apart from responding to specific enquiries from clients, the clients' skills were also assessed and information provided on the learning of new skills or the enhancing of existing ones.

The importance of attending a general business course such as the Private Enterprise Programme was always stressed throughout the consultation sessions to ensure that the client had an adequate knowledge of book-keeping, raising finance, business planning, and cash-flow. Business plans of existing small start-up clothing companies were given to clients to guide and help them. Any business plans prepared by the clients were checked to ensure the amounts allocated for equipment and materials were adequate and reasonable. Information was also given about various types of feasibility and start-up business grants available from local councils, The Prince's Trust and Task Force, for example. Clients were also told about any of the business advice agencies in their area providing 'Enterprise Rehearsal' facilities.

A few weeks of advice work was sufficient to enable the Project Coordinator to target the areas in which the client group needed most help. The clients were regularly 'sounded out' on the proposed programme and duration of training, and encouraged to give their views. Thus it was hoped that the training courses would provide a sound basis for meeting the specific needs of unemployed women starting their own clothing businesses. The first 'Start your own Clothing Business' training course began in March 1988. The number of participants on each course was intentionally kept low (below twelve) to create an informal atmosphere and to encourage active participation. To promote attendance on the course a child-care allowance was available. This was an important factor because the majority of the trainees were women, and a very high percentage of both the male and female trainees were unemployed.

Most of the training material was prepared with the assistance of specialist trainers and the technical staff of the Clothing Resource Centre. The training courses covered a range of subjects such as marketing, designing, sketching, sewing machines, sewing threads, costings, calculating 'mark-up' and premises (lease/licence regulations). Throughout the training courses specialist lecturers with extensive knowledge and experience of the clothing industry were used. The specialist lecturers therefore helped and trained the clients, not only to consider a range of issues and problems but also by showing them the best possible way to deal with these. In some of the sessions on each course, women already running small make-through clothing businesses were used to provide the training. They explained from first-hand experience how and why they started a business, the problems they encountered (for instance, limited finance), and most importantly, how they managed to overcome them. These sessions were usually the most popular because they enabled the clients to talk to someone who was 'in the same boat' and served as a source of encouragement to those who were on the first step of the ladder.

The courses achieved a good attendance rate, with a total of ninety-four clients benefiting from the training programme in the first year. These clients especially appreciated that the courses provided relevant information in a form which was tailor-made to meet their needs. For the women it also took account of their personal circumstances and their experiences as women trying to enter business.

A number of the businesses owned by women have made excellent progress. They are receiving bigger and better orders, and as a result require new staff. Those women who have successfully started businesses have required help and assistance at every stage and have contacted the Project Co-ordinator to seek advice and help in a number of areas: advice on fabrics, machinery, market research, costing, sourcing wholesalers of fashion garments, help with export and import regulations, importing yarns and fabrics, business insurance, self-employment and tax rules, VAT regulations and recruitment and training of staff. Some women who feel they are not yet ready to start their own business have been introduced to design orientated clothing businesses so that they can gain more experience by working for them.

Table 8.5 Progress of clients 1988-9 as at June 1989

Status	No.	%
Started business (i.e. trading)	98	50.52
Actively preparing to start business	16	8.24
Returned to employment	4	2.06
Unemployed	4	2.06
Business failed	1	0.52
No information	71	36.60
Total	194	100.00

Monitoring the progress of the first 194 clients was undertaken and Table 8.5 shows the results of this exercise.

Thirty-one clients were in business when they approached the Project for advice. With the help given the businesses were sustained. Sixty-seven new clothing businesses were assisted (see Richardson and Hartshorn this volume) and another sixteen businesses were supported to an advanced stage of pre-trading preparation. The majority of those who have not kept in contact with the Project have possibly decided not to pursue their business idea at this stage. This is not seen as a failure, either on the part of the Project or the individuals concerned. Self-employment does not suit everyone and it would be irresponsible to expect that everyone can be part of the new 'enterprise culture'. It is important to support unemployed people by fully investigating the viability (or non-viability) of their idea before they start trading. This approach helps to minimize the number of small business failures, which carry with them high indebtedness and loss of confidence. Unemployed people can ill afford these outcomes.

Notwithstanding this argument, however, some of those who have not yet started their own businesses may have potentially viable ideas and business plans, but face financial and attitudinal barriers, particularly from banks, other financial institutions and estate agents. Table 8.6 shows the distribution, by race and gender, of those who have started businesses.

According to the statistical monitoring, white clients have been more successful at establishing their businesses. Fifty-eight per cent of white males and 63 per cent of white females who consulted the Project are now self-employed. A slightly lower percentage of Asian male clients (55 per cent) are now also in this position. There is little difference between the proportions of Afro-Caribbean males (41 per cent) and Afro-Caribbean women (48 per cent) who are in self-employment. Asian women appear to be much less likely to have

Table 8.6 Trading businesses as at June 1989 by race and gender (numbers and percentage of each client group)

	Female	Male	Total
White	34 (63%)	7 (58%)	41 (62%)
Afro-Caribbean	26 (48%)	8 (41%)	34 (46%)
Asian	7 (30%)	16 (55%)	23 (44%)
Total	67 (50%)	31 (51%)	98 (51%)

entered business than their male counterparts, with only 30 per cent of them becoming self-employed.

These results suggest that the Project has enabled many unemployed people, including women and black people, to start businesses. However, women (most particularly Asian women) and black people still face significant barriers, in combating negative attitudes and raising finance. The Project has addressed these difficulties and in some cases has intervened in negotiations with providers of finance.

WOMEN WORKING FOR SUCCESS

We now turn to a number of case histories which highlight some of the problems and issues outlined above, and discuss the measures taken by the Clothing Resource Centre to assist these businesses.

Ann Smith, an older white woman, had been working part-time for a clothing company for a number of years and jointly owned a home with her husband. She had been advised by a business adviser and a financial adviser that the only way she could raise money to finance her business was by selling her house. No advice was given to her regarding the availability of any business grants or low interest rate loans from the local authority, or that instead of selling her house she could arrange a second mortgage to finance her business.

When she tried to find premises for the business (a retail shop) she was in most cases not sent any information by estate agents. Whenever she talked to them and expressed an interest in a particular property she felt they were only talking to her to 'keep her amused'. The property would be lying vacant for a number of weeks but as soon as she showed an interest there were suddenly several other people interested. The last shop that she had tried to rent was originally advertised for £3,500 p.a. This was then increased to £7,500 p.a. and finally to £15,000 p.a. just to put her off. A year afterwards, the shop still remained vacant. All this was happening against a background where the client had raised substantial finance for her business and had extensive knowledge of retailing and the products she was going to sell.

The Clothing Resource Centre helped Ann to locate and rent premises for her business and also assisted her with her application for 'New Business Start-Up' grants and a marketing grant from her local authority. The business she started is flourishing and has been operating for nearly two years, and her company has recently created two full-time jobs.

Jagdeep Kaur wanted to establish a small business to provide a freelance fashion design service. Doubts had been expressed by both the bank, and by the organization to whom she had applied for a grant to set up her business. The Clothing Resource Centre was contacted to give its expert opinion on her talent, skills, and the general viability of this type of business. With the assistance of the Centre she was successful with her application for the grant.

Delores King, a highly talented Afro-Caribbean designer and manufacturer of ladies' knitwear, needed financial assistance to market her range of products. With the help of the Clothing Resource Centre she was successful in her application for a grant from her local authority, which enabled her to take part in a National Ladieswear Trade Exhibition in London. On the first day she received orders worth just over £10,000. The business was home-based but assistance from the Clothing Resource Centre was sought to relocate into an industrial unit and to make an application for rent relief assistance. The company is in the process of creating one full-time and one part-time job.

Julie Thompson, a young white designer/manufacturer of highly specialized trimming for good quality ladies' wear, was supplied by the Clothing Resource Centre with the name and addresses of various department stores and chain stores where her goods could be sold, and she was also provided with marketing and packaging advice. She has been able to secure regular orders from one department store and a number of shops. She is seeking advice from the Clothing Resource Centre to help her to export the products to Canada and the USA.

These case histories represent only a small part of the specialized, and at times highly technical, advice and assistance the Clothing Resource Centre has provided to its clients. The need for specialist advice is exemplified by the fact that the Project Co-ordinator has been contacted on numerous occasions by women wishing to set up a business in sectors other than clothing (e.g. catering). Their enquiries are always to find out if there are other specialist business agencies to provide them with advice and training in their product sector. The answer, unfortunately, in almost all these cases has to be in the negative.

WHAT NEXT?

The work of the first twelve months of the Project helped to identify several areas which presented problems for women clients starting a clothing business. In addition to working with individual women, initiatives to address fabric sourcing, joint marketing and the establishment of a Business Club are being developed at the Clothing Resource Centre.

The Resource Centre has excellent sources of information about fabrics and fabric suppliers, but finding fabric wholesale suppliers who are willing to supply small quantities has proved extremely difficult. As in many other businesses, clothing companies in the start-up stage have limited working capital. Initially a company needs to manufacture a sample range to be shown to prospective buyers who then place orders for some or all of the garments in this range. In most cases fabric accounts for about 60 per cent of the cost of a garment. If the fabric is not bought from a wholesaler, but instead from a retail shop or a market stall, the manufacturing cost of a garment can become quite uncompetitive. In the West Midlands there are very few fabric wholesalers, and most of them stock a very limited variety of fabrics. Those which are stocked locally reflect the main products which have been manufactured in the area for a number of years (e.g. rainwear, jeans, and casual wear). Over the last few years many companies are increasingly finding that they have to diversify their products and are manufacturing better-designed garments using a variety of fashionable fabrics. Most of these manufacturers buy their stocks from manufacturers and wholesalers based in other parts of the UK, especially London or Manchester, or from abroad. To overcome at least some of these problems, one solution the Resource Centre is looking to develop is that of fabric co-operatives in the West Midlands. If a co-operative is able to stock a range of fabrics, at competitive prices, it is likely that many small, established clothing manufacturers as well as those just starting up would use this much needed service.

An interim and more immediate solution is for the Clothing Resource Centre to open accounts with various fabric wholesalers. After a great deal of gentle persuasion, a number of fabric suppliers have agreed to supply the Clothing Resource Centre's orders – whether large or small. To provide this service, the Centre will require clients to pay a small charge to cover the costs of administration. The Clothing Resource Centre will in future continue to strive to establish close contacts with fabric wholesalers and merchants in the UK and abroad.

For most small businesses, knowing how to market their products and the time and costs involved in marketing can present major problems. Many of the clients are very talented designers, or are excellent at sewing and designing, but in most cases have very little knowledge of the market, or are unaware of how to promote their products. In other cases, whilst the marketing knowledge is there, small businesses are unable to pursue the most appropriate marketing strategy, for example to employ a sales representative, due to lack of finance. A joint marketing venture could help to overcome a number of problems by reducing the costs of producing promotional literature and advertising, by providing technical marketing support, and by increasing awareness of the client's specialist market. The common mistake of undercharging for their products would not then be made, nor would it be used as a market-entry device (see Jones and Carter this volume).

To meet these needs the first clothing designers' marketing co-operative, Black Country Fashions, has been set up in Wolverhampton. The companies involved in the co-operative design and manufacture a wide range of garments, including evening wear, casual wear, lingerie, ladies' outsizes, and children's wear. Members of the co-operative, apart from running their own businesses, were selected to ensure that they also work as a group to produce both a range of co-ordinated garments and to manufacture each other's designs.

Soon after the co-operative was established, an opportunity arose for the group to open a retail shop in the heart of Wolverhampton's shopping centre. Wolverhampton Council helped the co-operative by providing rent-free shop premises for three months. The official launch of this Designer Show-Case Boutique received wide coverage in the local press, radio and television (including Central TV News), and this really helped to promote the co-operative. The opening of the shop enabled the group to test the market for their designs and gain valuable experience in retail management. The shop was staffed on a rota-basis, with two designers working in the shop each day. An enthusiastic response from the public to this made-to-measure designer service not only provided the co-operative members with good profits, but also helped to boost their confidence.

A number of well-known High Street retail chains were also contacted to find out if some kind of a link could be formed between them and the co-operative to raise its profile. The co-operative wanted to undertake joint promotion, publicity and advertising and maybe employ sales representatives or agents on a joint basis. The future plans of the co-operative include participation in trade exhibitions, such as the Harrogate Fashion Fair, joining Chamber of Commerce missions abroad and developing other joint marketing projects.

The establishment of the first designer clothing co-operative in Wolverhampton has shown the problems and complexities of setting up a joint venture of this type. However, the encouraging results are proving the need, popularity and viability of this type of umbrella organization for small companies. The Clothing Resource Centre has since been approached by several clients from different areas, who wish to set up similar joint-marketing ventures.

A large number of the women starting clothing businesses have expressed an interest in forming a Business Club at the Clothing Resource Centre, so that they could meet other people with a similar outlook and problems. Whilst attending training courses at the Clothing Resource Centre many clients form close links, provide help and share information with each other. Already a system of 'networking' has developed whereby clients buy from each other to supplement their own designer range or jointly work with other small businesses.

Most of the women complained that they feel very isolated working from home or a small industrial unit. They feel that regular contact with other small businesses who are facing similar problems to themselves would be extremely useful. The Business Club would meet regularly and, apart from providing a networking facility, could organize specialist seminars on topics of general interest, such as how to organize a successful Party-Plan, and could hold video slide shows of the latest styles, design, and colour predictions from France, Italy, London and elsewhere.

Exchange of information, moral support, and self-help will be the basis of this Business Club. It is hoped that those clothing businesses who have managed to get over the birth-pains of starting a business and have set up a successful enterprise could help other clients contemplating doing the same. Established make-through clothing business owners can, therefore, act as role-models and mentors for those women who are starting a business and help them with their development and growth.

CONCLUSION

Government advertisements in the press and media for the Enterprise Allowance Scheme generally give the impression that starting a business is glamorous and easy. In the real world this image could not be further from the truth. Many people do not have the right temperament, motivation or determination to set up a business; and for some people it is simply a desperate attempt to find a way out of the misery and degradation of the dole queues.

When a woman decides to set up a business she needs business related and sector specific information, advice and training. In many cases unemployed people do not have even a basic knowledge of the market or of the competition. There is a great variety of general agencies providing general business advice and training. Sometimes a business or enterprise agency has an adviser on its staff, who has been seconded from a company or organization with experience and knowledge of a specialized market. This is very much a 'hit and miss' approach and cannot guarantee that a client would receive advice that is both of high quality and is sector specific. There have been many cases, for instance, where a garment is beautifully designed, but is not made to the right quality or standard or which is not produced in the right fabric or right colours for the season. It may not be costed accurately or be being sold in the appropriate market. Any one of these factors or a combination of them can, and often does, lead to a small clothing business producing very little, if any, profit and in some cases failing to survive at all.

The women clients using the Project brought with them on some occasions very professional looking business plans, produced with the help of business advice agencies. Frequently they did not really understand what had been written in the business plan or the meaning of the cash-flow projections. As the business advisers in most cases lack the specialist technical and marketing knowledge about a particular product, the women are unable to give the best impression of their product or business idea in their business plan. This in turn creates a situation where, if asked any technical questions about the product, idea or service in an interview, the client is unable to answer in a confident and convincing manner. Such matters are extremely important, especially when trying to raise finance for the business.

To compound this problem of credibility further, many women from the inner city trying to start-up in business also face negative racial and gender stereotyping by banks, estate agents, and other financial institutions as to their competence to run a business. To some of these professionals, clothing and other home-based or craft businesses are still seen as more of a hobby when women are involved than as a serious business proposition. The need for specialist business advice to meet the needs of unemployed women has been proved by the large number of such clients who have received advice, support, and training at the Clothing Resource Centre and by the excellent support the project has received from local councils, organizations, and agencies concerned about these issues. The combination of craft skill, subsidized income for a year, and one-day enterprise awareness course is definitely not adequate or appropriate to start a business in a highly competitive market such as that of clothing. Not only has the Project shown the need for specialist business support, advice, and training but it has demonstrated how this can be met. The needs of inner city residents entering clothing self-employment are determined by two main factors. First, the nature of the clothing industry, particularly in terms of market trends and specific technical processes is such that general management, including production management skills, are not a sufficient basis on which to start a successful business. Second, women and particularly black women, who tend to comprise the majority of individuals wishing to start clothing businesses, face discrimination of various kinds and are not taken seriously by many existing business advisors and bank managers. The Project represents a successful and innovative approach to tackling, in a practical way, both sets of problems.

ACKNOWLEDGEMENTS

The Business Start-Up Project would not have been possible without the personal support of Joe Montgomery, then Assistant Secretary of the Barrow and Geraldine S. Cadbury Trust; Geoff Vaughan, then Manager of the West Midlands Clothing Resource Centre and Kevin Maton of the West Midlands Enterprise Board. The success of the Project is in a large part due to the commitment and enthusiasm of the women and men who are determined to explore self-employment in the clothing industry. We would also like to thank all our current colleagues for their support in completing this chapter, but especially Mo Johal for her typing.

9 Good practice in business advice and counselling

Carole Truman

SMALL BUSINESS SUPPORT NETWORKS

Throughout the 1980s there was a growth in the range of different support agencies for small businesses. By the end of the decade, it was estimated that every person in Britain lived within ten miles of a local enterprise agency (Business in the Community 1989). Although not the only form of support and counselling open to the small business owner, the exponential growth of local enterprise agencies (LEAs) led to them becoming an important feature of enterprise support networks.

Counselling of people wishing to start-up a small business is a core activity of all LEAs. In addition, they may also provide training courses, exhibitions, newsletters, small business clubs, loan fund management, and workspace. Besides LEAs, others providing support to new businesses include co-operative development agencies; specialist agencies for young people, black people, and the unemployed; independent support services; banks and accountants. All provide particular types of support to client groups. LEAs are an important resource, however, because they are funded through partnerships between the public and private sectors to deliver a broad generic service to small business owners within their catchment area.

This chapter is based upon a piece of empirical research which took a detailed look at twenty-two LEAs across the country.[1] The main purpose of the research was to identify measures and innovations which have been shown to improve the accessibility of LEAs to women in business. It should be emphasized from the outset that the purpose of the chapter is not to provide a critical assessment of LEAs in relation to their accessibility and appropriateness to women entrepreneurs. Instead, it will examine the scope and limitations of enterprise and other agencies in providing support which is focused on the particular and various needs of women entering small business.

122 *Women in business*

The chapter begins with an outline of ways in which specific support services might be targeted to meet the needs of women. It then goes on to consider the limitations that are faced by individual support agencies in meeting women's needs. Ultimately, a dilemma is posed which outlines the tensions between providing support and advice in the short-term, and other factors which influence women's experience of running small businesses over time.

WOMEN AS CLIENTS OF SUPPORT NETWORKS

Businesses are considerably more likely to succeed if they take advantage of support offered by business advice and development agencies. If women's businesses are to share in this measure of success, it is vital that support organizations are equipped and able to meet their needs. There is increasing evidence that women have particular needs when they go into self-employment (see Richardson and Hartshorn this volume). Some recommend that help and advice for women is best provided by women counsellors. Indeed there is a strong case which proposes that women need their own separate business advice agencies. Where these exist, they have been shown to offer an effective and comprehensive support service that is orientated specifically to meet women's needs. However, there are also many ways in which generic LEAs can make efforts to improve the service. that they offer to women.

The section which follows describes ways in which the services of LEAs may be tuned to identify and meet the needs of female clients. It begins by discussing the importance of gathering adequate monitoring information to assess if all potential clients are being reached. Methods of marketing the agency to women are then described, followed by a discussion of particular initiatives such as the use of outreach work or special exhibitions. There is then a discussion of the type and content of counselling that might be appropriate to women's needs. Business clubs for women and support and advocacy that is oriented towards women's needs are another aspect of support provision. Finally, attention is given to the provision of training for women.

MONITORING INFORMATION

The introduction to this volume discusses the possibility of how the proportion of women starting in business at present exceeds that of men. The collation of national statistics is problematic, but even at a local level evidence is scarce on the proportion of women who use enterprise agencies. Several forms of monitoring are undertaken by all LEAs, but the gender of clients is not always recorded in monitoring data or their annual reports. Of the agencies which do monitor their clients by gender, women usually form only a small minority of clients.

If quantitative data are scarce, even less evidence exists to evaluate the quality of support that LEAs provide for women. There would appear to be an urgent need for LEAs to monitor the number of women who use the agency network. Statistics may not provide any assessment of the quality of service that is provided by an LEA, but monitoring by gender is one crucial indicator of the effectiveness of coverage of a local community. An approximate indicator of the quality or relevance of the service offered by agencies might be to monitor the rate of repeat visits by gender.

Monitoring will be carried out only if there are clear incentives to do so. In practice, there appears to be little evidence that the sponsors and the boards of agencies have included gender within their monitoring criteria. This is crucial, since funding agents undoubtedly have greatest leverage to ask for monitoring to be undertaken.

The current practice of many agencies is merely to undertake a head-count of clients who use various services. At its most extreme, this basic approach to monitoring could result in agencies logging all telephone calls (including wrong numbers). This type of information may well be an indicator of how busy the staff of agencies are, but it fails fundamentally to identify who are the actual clients. It may not be sufficient to declare that an agency is booked up for months ahead and must therefore be successful. The reality may be that only a small sector of the local community is actually in touch with the agency, whilst large sections of potential clients are being missed. In such circumstances it seems important to identify the various client groups within the community and devise ways of marketing the agency to them.

The purpose of more comprehensive monitoring is not necessarily to increase the number of clients who use an agency, but instead to identify whether there is a need to broaden the base of clients who may potentially benefit from the services of the agency. If in practice this leads to an increase in the number of clients, then agencies would be in a strong position to ask for more support to meet the needs of these clients.

The criteria by which agencies evaluate their success could change to encompass issues that would be of benefit to female clients. For example, one such agency found that women require more long-term support than their male equivalents. Monitoring information was used to gain sponsorship for a women-only branch of the agency.

If the criteria for monitoring were broadened to encompass those which took women into account, agencies would be in a better position to become more pro-active and to identify the needs of the local community.

MARKETING SERVICES TO WOMEN

Most agencies collect information about how their clients first came to hear of their service. In the agencies which were visited during this research, word of mouth and information at job centres were two of the most common forms of referral. Word of mouth is an important form of marketing which suggests that once women begin to make better use of agencies, so more women will begin to hear of the agency if the service which is provided is appropriate to their needs. On the other hand, if women do not hear about agencies from alternative sources, then it is possible that they may be excluded from word of mouth networks. For this reason, agencies need to take specific initiatives to locate women.

The marketing of services to women needs to begin by locating where women are. In one agency the first step in marketing was seen to be the most important and this meant locating women in the community. A female employee of the agency believed that women were less likely to respond to an advertisement in the local paper than they might to a poster on the wall of a children's clinic or doctor's surgery. Efforts were made to identify new ways of reaching women. Other agencies have made efforts to contact local groups such as play groups or church groups. This type of contact often falls outside traditional agency links.

Several agencies have attracted press coverage for businesses run by women. This has the benefit of raising the profile of the work of the agency and also of promoting positive images of business women. Likewise, agency promotional material *should* also feature women and women's businesses. In several agencies, efforts have been made to ensure that the agency magazine included photographs of women or that a feature was made of a business run by a woman. Promotional material of this type can have a wide circulation and can provide a positive image of the agency's ability to meet the needs of diverse groups. In another agency, sponsorship was sought to design and produce a leaflet and booklet orientated towards particular target groups.

OUTREACH WORK

A comment that has frequently been raised in LEAs is that many of the women who come in as clients have already thought through their business plans to a great extent before they come to the office. In some cases, this has been put forward as an argument that women do not need extra support from agencies. However, unless monitoring figures support the notion that the number of women using the agency match the number of men, then there is the possibility of self-selection amongst women using the agency. That is to say that the agency may in practice be accessible to men who are at any stage of putting together a business plan, whereas women tend not to come forward until they are more confident that they have a good, well thought through idea. If women are to enjoy equal access to agencies, efforts must be made to 'broaden the trawl' of clients. Several agencies have used various forms of outreach work to do this.

In some cases, agencies have received support for community based initiatives or outreach work and as a consequence have found that more women have begun to use the agency even where the initiative was not aimed specifically at women. Outreach work operates more closely with the community than an office base can allow and so it is particularly relevant to women.

Where a worker is employed specifically to undertake outreach work, efforts can be made to make contact with existing groups. This may be through existing community groups and networks. The aim might be to gain and build confidence within the local community and to help define its needs. Development work may include visits to local businesses and devising training programmes. Some outreach workers may also spend one morning a week at job centres or in shopping centres. There are many examples of LEAs using outreach workers and it is also possible to learn from the experiences of outreach work in other community organizations which operate in similar settings. Other local services, for example health services, community education, and so on, may also be able to pass on experience of doing outreach work within a particular community.

Outreach work does not necessarily need a formal outreach worker – even from an office base many agencies found it possible to provide talks to groups in the evenings or at lunchtimes about setting up a small business. There is always scope to broaden the range of groups who are addressed by such talks.

Another branch of outreach work that has been used by agencies has been in response to the need of some groups to know how benefits will be affected by going into self-employment. Women in particular may be caught in the 'poverty trap' whereby if they begin to earn money they lose social security benefits. In such circumstances, self-employment has to be seen in a broad context and an agency needs to have access to other advice services such as the Citizens' Advice Bureau.

One of the problems that agencies have associated with outreach work is how to evaluate its success. Because of its grass roots nature, outreach is an evolutionary process and does not show instant results. In some cases, the private sector has been reluctant to invest in such work. This is another LEA issue which funding bodies need to address.

SPECIAL EVENTS

A number of agencies have received one-off grants to organize events aimed specifically at raising the profile of women in business. The example of a 'Women Mean Business' exhibition and conference is one which could be developed. Commonly, one result of the interest shown in such events is that they serve as a stimulus for others to organize similar events in successive years. Spin-off initiatives such as women-only training courses and a women's business club can become part of the agency's activities.

A sponsor-led approach can be extremely influential in providing an incentive to develop work with women, but there must also be an onus on agencies to seek out sponsorship for such events.

CONTENT AND QUALITY OF COUNSELLING AND ADVICE

In the agencies contacted during this research, it was agreed that women need access to the same help and advice as men. It was also agreed that counselling sessions involving women may follow a different pattern and that the help and advice that was sought might be asked for in different ways. In one agency, it was recognized that women's approach to seeking advice was best met by an advice agency orientated specifically to meet their needs and a sponsorship package was found to enable a sister agency to operate alongside the existing LEA.

In another agency, the ambience of the agency was seen to be important in helping people from all backgrounds to feel at ease. It was felt that if everyone in the agency wore business suits it would not provide the right atmosphere. Many agencies recognized that women may have had to pluck up considerable courage to come to get advice. Simple actions, such as offering everyone a cup of coffee, can help to make them feel at ease.

Most agencies agreed that women counsellors should be available to provide advice to both male and female clients to ensure that advice for women by women does not exist in a ghetto. The issue of female business advisers is discussed later.

The overriding impression from discussions about what type of advice is appropriate for women was that there needs to be a sensitivity to the needs and circumstances of the individual. So whilst some counsellors mentioned how they would advise on child care, others said it should only be discussed if raised by the women themselves – otherwise they would assume the client has taken the issue on board. In a general sense, a good counselling approach for women may not differ from the requirements for good counselling generally. Counsellors said they could never assume that they understand the needs of clients, but would use the counselling sessions to help identify these.

A good counselling approach will be good both for men and for women. This is not the same as saying everybody should be treated the same – both men and women need to be helped to recognize the skills they have, but in a society where women's skills are undervalued counsellors may need to adopt a particular approach to help women to recognize their strengths and weaknesses. Thus a woman may describe herself as a housewife, which at first sight will disguise the skills that household management involves, such as time management, budgeting, interpersonal skills, and so on. Counsellors may need training to be helped to recognize women's experience so that they can provide appropriate counselling to female clients. Women's business advice agencies such as The Women's Enterprise Development Agency (WEDA) and networks such as Women in Enterprise have already developed considerable expertise in this area.

LEAs described how many women by necessity choose to operate in business sectors that are easy to access but produce low profits. Part of the role of agencies might be to recognize the limitations on women's choices and offer support to help women raise their sights and explore new business areas. This point is developed below.

SUPPORT AND ADVOCACY

One major problem that has been cited by women is the issue of gaining credibility by professionals such as bank managers and accountants (see Koper this volume). Black women face the additional obstacle of racism when they appear in a bank manager's office with no evidence of a track record in business (see Kaur and Hayden this volume). The counsellors in our research reported very few instances of anyone being turned away by bank managers if they had a good business plan. The quintessence of the problem appears to be ensuring that people are not despatched to the bank unless they are well prepared, and agencies must recognize the importance of their role in assisting the preparation of good business plans. There were a number of isolated instances of people being refused support which advisers believed they deserved. In such cases, most advisers said they would be prepared to act as an advocate on behalf of their clients. The overriding philosophy seemed to be that prevention was better than a cure. But business advisers can help further by insisting that banks provide women with reasons for not granting a loan. Women may not have the confidence to approach a bank that has given them a negative response and may never discover why their application was turned down.

BUSINESS CLUBS

On-going support and self-help can be provided by a business club. Many examples of successful business clubs for women can be found. One business club emerged following a successful conference and exhibition on women's business. It was recognized that there was a need to provide on-going support for women business owners. A local sponsor provided a free buffet and city centre premises so that the club could meet every month. The business club was a way of maintaining the contact for exhibitors as well as for other women in business in the locality.

Such meetings can also provide support and role models for women who are new in business, or perhaps just thinking about starting up (see Kaur and Hayden this volume). In this particular example, the city centre location meant that the meetings were easily accessible to women from different parts of the area. Women were able to share experiences of running a business and offer support and advice on a whole range of issues. Such groups may be addressed by outside speakers, or meetings can be organized around single themes so that women learn through talking to each other.

PROVISION OF TRAINING

It has been argued that training may be seen to be successful if it provides an individual with the confidence to undertake a task about which they had previously not felt confident. Training practitioners have identified a strong need to include confidence building and assertiveness as well as business skills in training courses for women. The hours over which the course runs should also be adapted to fit in with women's commitments and a creche or child care allowance should be available (see Richardson and Hartshorn this volume). Such elements are rarely included in mixed sex training programmes. Single sex training has been shown to enable more women to take up business ownership because it can provide a supportive environment not only during the course, but also links can be maintained after a course. Women benefit from such courses even if they do not go on to set up their own business. Several agencies had developed women-only training courses and whilst many were still classified as 'experimental', most had proved to be very popular and were commonly oversubscribed.

The demand for women-only training can be met given that there is continued funding to facilitate them. In some cases, the local office of the Training Commission (TC) had provided the impetus to develop women-only training. However, changes in the structure and priorities of the TC mean that continued support for training has not always been forthcoming. An Equal Opportunities Conference (EOC 1988) identified a need to develop a flexible standard model course equivalent to the Business Enterprise Programme which could attract consistent funding and which might lead to accreditation as adult vocational education. Further issues relating to training are discussed in the chapters by Richardson and Hartshorn, and Kaur and Hayden in this volume.

Another idea put forward by a number of LEAs was to develop training courses for husband and wife partnerships. This was in response to an acknowledgement that a woman frequently makes a significant contribution to the success of her husband's business, but may not receive recognition for the work she does. Partnership training could formalize the woman's involvement by making her a more equal partner and so preventing the woman's contribution being hidden.

LEAs which have a commitment to encouraging more women into business should consider developing training provision aimed specifically at women.

LIMITS TO THE INFLUENCE OF SUPPORT NETWORKS

Existing research recommends that if women are to benefit from the services of LEAs to an equal extent to men, then initiatives need to be taken which are tailored to meet their needs as a target group. This can take place only if resources are initiated or redeployed to take account of women's needs. This has implications for the management of existing resources within agencies and for initiatives which are promoted by the funding bodies of LEAs.

It should be stressed that so far this chapter has highlighted some of the ways in which agencies may meet women's needs which may differ from those of men. Many differences occur because women's life experiences contrast with those of men in terms of the education they receive, their involvement with their families, their levels of confidence, the social spaces which they occupy and the circles in which they mix. That most women have responsibilities for children or elderly or sick relatives is an integral fact of their lives which needs to be taken into account. However, not all women have child care commitments and yet may still share other characteristics of women as a social group who are or aspire to be in business. As Kaur and Hayden (this volume) point out, other groups of women, such as those from ethnic minorities, face different obstacles when setting up businesses and may have additional needs.

A concern has been expressed that the development of good practice in LEAs and the promotion of positive action directs resources away from existing activities in order to provide privileges for women. There is no evidence to support this concern but agencies do need to recognize the particular characteristics of women as target groups and ensure that the services which are offered are in tune with women's different needs.

Our research revealed several perspectives on how agencies perceived their abilities to identify and meet the specific and various needs of women. There was an agreement amongst staff at LEAs that they should provide counselling and advice to women but there were differing views about how this might be achieved. Some held that women should have equal access to any help provided by business advice agencies. Others believed that provision should be oriented specifically towards the needs of women and that women's experiences were sufficiently different to men's to warrant separate provision.

Our findings suggest that in practice, women who are contemplating self employment would encounter one of three types of agency:

1 The first type holds that there is nothing to prevent women from using their service: they believe that if women fail to seek their help it cannot be the fault of the agency. In this situation, there is probably no incentive for the agency to alter its *modus operandi*, since the criteria by which the success of the agency is judged rests on its existing client base without explicit reference to women.
2 The second type report that the women they see are usually better prepared in terms of their business idea than men. At face value such agencies may be proud of their female client base. Whilst this may show the agency has some understanding of issues which women face, it may disguise the fact that female clients are in reality being more self-selecting than men, for whom self-employment is merely one option to try. The competing demands which women experience mean that they need to be more realistic about what they expect from self-employment. Before a woman decides to go to a business advice agency, she may well have thought through many of the prospects and limitations of being self-employed. For these women there is no need to use LEA counsellors to talk through the realities of what self-employment might offer. Instead, they are more likely to be concerned with the more straightforward practical issues which need to be confronted.
3 The third type, the minority of agencies, know that to help women start up in business requires a recognition of their position in society. As such, they see the need to provide women-only training to assist with personal development needs. These agencies also frequently acknowledge that women's circumstances are such that the best help they can give is to enable women to reach a decision to defer or even give up the idea of starting a business. In other words, the vulnerability of small business owners is such that they can easily exploit themselves and so work all hours to repay loans and earn a decent standard of living. Kaur and Hayden (this volume) describe the kind of commitment within local economies that is required to overcome these barriers.

The third category of agency seems to have a realistic assessment of the prospects for women's businesses but clearly it is beyond the scope of LEAs, acting in isolation, to remedy these problems. Our research suggests that despite the growth of the small business support network, the potential for improvements in the prospects for women entering self-employment is limited. The way that support agencies have been established and organized suggests that many have a limited understanding of women's position in the labour market and the issues that they face when trying to generate an income from self-employment. Among those which do show some understanding there seems to be an implicit assumption that the marginalisation and vulnerability of the self-employed mean that it is not an option that women should undertake lightly.

It appears from our investigation that many support agencies have become institutionalized in a way that services the needs of the self-employed person provided he is a man. As such, unless they form strong partnerships within local economies, they can do little more than support and re-reinforce existing labour market structures which favour men and marginalize women.

NOTE

1 This was part of the Women in Business Enterprise project at the University of Bradford, funded by the Leverhulme Trust.

10 Women's businesses in Europe
EEC initiatives

Caroline Turner

This chapter seeks to provide a profile of enterprise creation by women across the EEC in the 1980s and to analyse the appropriateness to their needs of existing sources of business support. The focus is on small business creation, particularly by women who are disadvantaged in terms of access to the labour market and for whom small enterprise creation is often the only way out of unemployment.

The chapter starts by outlining the growth in women's enterprise creation over the past decade and draws attention to EC-level studies that highlight key characteristics of women and their businesses and the support available to them. A more detailed picture is given of the sectoral trends of women's enterprise and their motivations for business start-up.

The main focus is on sources of support for business creation, at member-state and EC levels. Conventional support mechanisms for both male and female entrepreneurs are evaluated in terms of their appropriateness to the needs of women starting small businesses and recommendations for improvements are made. Information and advice, training and financial services directed specifically at women entrepreneurs are discussed and reference made to networks of women's businesses and their support agents. The work and experiences of the European Commission programme in support of women's enterprise initiatives is analysed in some detail, leading into the concluding section, in which areas for future action are indicated.

BACKGROUND

Although statistical data are sparse and incomplete, research, together with meetings and experience over the past decade have highlighted female entrepreneurship as a growing phenomenon across the member states of the European Community. For instance, it is estimated that women now account for about one in three enterprise creators in Germany and Denmark, one in four in France, the UK and The Netherlands and one in five in Greece, Spain, Italy and Ireland. To give some more specific examples, it is estimated that since 1981 self-employment among women in the UK has increased by some 68 per cent (Howieson 1988). In Germany, levels of self-employment have been rising over the 1980s, with the proportion of women among the self-employed increasing by over 3 per cent between 1974 and 1987 (Haas and Nesemann 1988), while in Greece, women as a proportion of all self-employed increased from 12 per cent to 18 per cent, in the decade 1976–86 (Turner and Papioannou 1988).

Initial EC-level research on women's business creation has brought to light key characteristics of women and their enterprises, and the support available to them (Turner 1989).

SECTORAL TRENDS

Studies of the sectoral development of women's enterprise initiatives in the Community demonstrate a predominance in the tertiary sector, as well as a concentration in the so-called 'traditionally female' branches of the economy (Halpern and Szurek 1989). Thus, women's businesses are most commonly found in hotel and catering, personal and social services, administrative and business services, retailing, textiles, ready-to-wear clothing and crafts. The concentration of women's businesses in the service sector can be placed against the background of women's participation in employment more generally. It is estimated that 73 per cent of women in employment in the EC work in the service sector, compared to 60 per cent of the working population. In the 1960s less than 40 per cent of the total working population were occupied in the service sector (Commission of European Communities 1989).

This overall picture of the sectoral trends in women's enterprise development suggests, on the one hand, that women are creating businesses in fields where they feel comfortable on the basis of their experiences in employment and/or the household. On the other hand, however, it conceals the *innovative* elements that characterize many women's enterprises. These include innovation in the context of 'traditionally female branches', through the creation of a new product or service for a particular market, such as organic catering services, manufacture of natural health care products, multicultural child care provisions. 'Green' business is a field in which the presence of women's enterprise is strong, through initiatives such as environmental counselling, ecological farming, and recycling of waste products. Nevertheless women's enterprise is not absent from either high-technology fields, such as advanced business and information systems services, or from male-dominated branches such as the manual trades (Turner 1990).

In addition, women's enterprises often demonstrate innovation of a less tangible, qualitative kind in their approach to entrepreneurship and working relations. They display creativity, flexibility, a human and personal approach to business management, attention to social and cultural goals, not just financial ones, in the running of their businesses.

MOTIVATIONS

The extent and nature of business creation by women in the regions of the Community vary according to factors related to economic, political, and socio-cultural configurations, particularly in relation to policies, attitudes, and traditions in the fields of enterprise and women's work. Personal factors clearly also play a role. Women entrepreneurs are by no means a homogeneous group. Their backgrounds, motivations, and the difficulties they face vary, as do the types and extent of support to which they have access. However, in general, the factors contributing to the growth in female entrepreneurship across the Community during the 1980s can be broadly divided into 'push' and 'pull' elements (see also Epstein in this volume).

The increasing proportion of women seeking paid work, especially those wishing to combine paid employment with family responsibilities and those seeking to return to work after a break have, within a context of rapid technological developments and structural changes in the labour market, contributed to the rise in female unemployment. In 1989, according to Eurostat women constituted over half of the unemployed, (52.4 per cent) and 55 per cent of the long-term unemployed in the Community as a whole. Thus, against the background of rising unemployment, underemployment, and unstable or unsatisfactory job conditions and prospects, a growing number of women have been 'pushed' into creating their own jobs through setting up small businesses. Many factors have 'pulled' women into entrepreneurship nevertheless, including personal ambition, creativity, a desire for independence – to be one's own boss, self-realization and an ambition to improve the quality of working conditions, to raise economic returns, and to develop a flexibility that caters for the combination of family responsibilities with gainful employment.

In general, the characteristics of women 'pushed' into business creation differ from those of women 'pulled' into entrepreneurship. The first case includes women facing particular difficulties in gaining access to the labour market, such as long-term unemployed women, those with limited or outdated skills, women in regions of limited job opportunity such as inner cities and rural areas, socially-disadvantaged women such as lone parents, migrants, ethnic minorities and the disabled. These women often lack sufficient start-up funds, have limited education and/or specific training, lack appropriate business experience, know-how, contacts, and self-confidence. In contrast, women who choose entrepreneurship often have backgrounds, resources, and experience conducive to 'successful' development of their own enterprise, within the conventional business environment. They are women with high levels of education, with experience in responsible salaried employment positions, with family enterprise traditions and contact networks.

SUPPORT

Just as the characteristics, motivations, and backgrounds of women entrepreneurs vary, so their support needs differ, both quantitatively and qualitatively. Support available to women starting small businesses varies in type and extent between the member states of the EC. In some cases, such as in Italy, France, Germany, and the UK, local and regional level structures, both public and private, occupy an important place in the overall support for women's enterprise initiatives. In others, such as Greece, Portugal and Ireland, this support tends to be restricted to a limited number of mainly public, national structures, offering mixed male/female rather than gender-specific provisions. These conventional support bodies are rarely attuned to the needs of women setting up enterprises, in terms of business size and sector (see Kaur and Hayden, Richardson and Hartshorn, Truman this volume).

Despite variations between member states, it is possible to present an overview of support provisions for entrepreneurs in the Community, specifically as they relate to the needs of women, and to draw out examples of initiatives that target women enterprise creators in particular. For the purposes of analysis and clarity, forms of support are discussed under four main headings: information and advice, training, funding, and networks.

Information and advice

Public and private organizations offering advice and information to entrepreneurs exist in all member states – such as Chambers of Commerce, Euro-Info Centres, Small and Medium-Sized Enterprise (SME) support agencies, business consultancy firms, and so on. Similarly, formal organizations concerned with the issues of equal opportunities exist across the Community, whose work includes provision of information and advice to women. However, in very few cases do these two types of provision come together, in the form of enterprise information and advice services specifically addressed to women. Where such facilities do exist, they usually spring from independent initiatives that are local or regional rather than nationwide.

Examples of initiatives offering information and advice specifically to women starting businesses include the Regional Development Agency for Women's Enterprise in Berlin, Frauenbetriebe in Frankfurt, Frau und Arbeit in Hamburg, Stirling Council EDU and several enterprise trusts in Scotland, The Women's Enterprise Development Agency in Birmingham, Women and Work Centres in the Netherlands, the Centre for Women's Employment Initiatives in Greece, Associazione Donna e Sviluppo in Italy, Central Tecnic Dona and Women's World Banking in Spain, CNIDFF (Paris) via regional and local level officers, as well as locally based women's initiatives in some parts of France such as 'Initielles' in the Midi-Pyrenees and Women and Enterprise in Nanterre.

What is common to many of these information and advice services targeting women entrepreneurs is their table d'hôte approach, but with an à la carte facility. That is to say, they offer a support package that combines various forms of assistance, but that has an in built flexibility to cater effectively for the differing needs and requirements of individual women entrepreneurs.

Why is it that gender-specific business support services should be developing? What is it about conventional business information and consultancy services that do not meet the needs of many women setting up small enterprises?

Research has revealed that women starting small enterprises often remain isolated from business information and advice, which is a basic stage in the entrepreneurial process (Turner 1989). This is due partly to a lack of targeting of women with business information and consultancy services, available at clear points of reference at local/regional level. Women are, in addition, often alienated by the orientation of the services, which tend to be based on the needs and approach of male entrepreneurs, whose starting point is often very different from that of their female counterparts. The differences include training and work experience, availability of personal funds, know-how in the ways of the business world, personal attitudes to entrepreneurship and size and sector of business.

Moreover, advisers are often male and orientated towards the needs of larger businesses, with little understanding or recognition of the specific obstacles faced by women starting up their own business, such as home–professional conflicts, limited capital and collateral, little if any management training or experience, lack of business relations and of access to networks created by and for men, where business contacts and deals are often made.

Thus, conventional sources of business information and advice tend to be orientated towards the reality, motivations, and background of male entrepreneurs, with the result that many women feel these services do not address their needs and thus they are discouraged from using them. As we have observed in the foregoing, business advisory services tailored specifically to women entrepreneurs are few and far between in the Community as a whole, such that the specific requirements of many women taking enterprise initiatives remain inadequately catered for by existing services.

There is an essential need for detailed and specific studies. The paucity of gender-specific research on the appropriateness of existing services both reflects and is a product of male orientation in these, like other, business support structures.

Detailed research on the information, counselling, and consultancy needs of different 'types' of women entrepreneur (returners, young qualified but inexperienced, unskilled), together with systematic monitoring and evaluation of existing services in relation to these needs would form a concrete basis for defining inadequacies and formulating new strategies for the effective and appropriate support of women starting their own businesses. Access to information and advice is a vital preliminary stage in the entrepreneurial process.

Coordinated efforts by small business support centres and equal opportunities bodies working at local level are required, to create business information and advice services that appropriately target women and meet their needs. Outreach services, such as have been operated by the Women's Enterprise Development Agency in Birmingham (UK) and a freephone for women entrepreneurs, offered in Ireland in the past, are examples of measures that can reduce the isolation of women starting businesses, especially those outside urban centres.

Awareness-creation within conventional business advice services, on the particular obstacles women face and on the special qualities they can bring to the entrepreneurial process, is vitally important. An essential ingredient of such a programme is the projection of realistic role models to give confidence to women and raise the profile of female entrepreneurship. In addition, training of advisory staff in order that their professional skills and personal approach are appropriate to the needs of women entrepreneurs is required. Awareness campaigns addressed to women, through publications and media, to encourage them to consider entrepreneurship and to attract them to support programmes are also needed.

Training

The type and extent of training available to women setting up businesses varies within and between member states. While most entrepreneurs can access some form of business training, these opportunities are often regionally restricted, while courses specifically addressed to women are severely limited. The situation is even more discouraging when it comes to pre-training and post start-up courses in various aspects of business development.

Although homemaking, of which many women have experience, relies on the performance of many managerial functions, such as planning, organizing, directing, mediating, negotiating, training is required if the link between home and enterprise is to be made effectively. The experience many women have as employees often does not offer them the opportunity to develop specific management skills and business know-how, while those returning to work after a break have often lost skills and/or confidence in the interim, which sets them back a pace when it comes to creating their own business.

Thus, and for other reasons related to the gender socialization process, the starting point and approach to entrepreneurship of many women differs from that of men. Mixed male/female training courses, whose content and methods tend to be based on the needs and approach of male entrepreneurs, do not always meet the requirements of women starting an enterprise, particularly in relation to the development of personal skills and the recognition of their life experience as a starting point for business training. In addition, experience suggests that the presence and attitudes of men on training courses can inhibit equal and active participation by women. Use of women trainers drawing upon experienced women entrepreneurs have demonstrated positive effects.

In response to the particular needs of women starting businesses and the deficiencies of many mixed training courses, specific training programmes for women have been developing in some regions of the Community in recent years. Examples of such initiatives, which have a local/regional rather than nationwide spread, include: Women's World Banking and Progetto Donna Artigiane in Italy, the Anne Polakschool in The Netherlands, Keys to Employment in Belgium, Frauenbetriebe and Grundungsrausch in Germany, The Women's Enterprise Development Agency, New Working Women, and the Women's Enterprise Unit of the Scottish Enterprise Foundation in the UK, the Aarhus Enterprise Centre and Vejle County in Denmark, and IEFP in Portugal.

The initiative for many of these training programmes has sprung from individual women or groups with experience of and sensitivity to the needs of women entrepreneurs. In some cases, they have been successful in gaining financial support from local, national or EC sources, but this is usually restricted in time and/or type of activity, with little development of such courses on a long-term and systematic basis.

An integrated and flexible approach is the hallmark of women-only training courses. Using the existing capabilities and experiences of each woman as a starting point, courses are flexible in order to fulfil individual as well as shared needs, often combining business and personal skill development, such as self-confidence, presentation and negotiation skills, and assertiveness.

Despite these encouraging examples, training opportunities that specifically target women setting up businesses are still nonexistent in many regions and sparse in the Community as a whole. There is a need for the systematic development of both pre-training and enterprise training opportunities targeting women and geared to their specific needs which are available systematically on a local/regional basis, and which take account of market and sectoral trends in the context of the European Single Market. Specific modules need to be formulated around the particular needs of different groups of women, according to their background, experience, motivations and aims, catering for different stages in the enterprise development cycle. Technical training programmes that enable women entrepreneurs to develop new skills and update existing ones, in line with market and sectoral developments, are also needed. Post-training follow-up support, such as apprenticeships, business 'nurseries', networking, and consultancy, would help women overcome pitfalls in the tough start-up phase.

A two-pronged approach is recommended to improve the quantity and quality of enterprise training for women. On the one hand, mixed male/female training schemes need to be evaluated in relation to the appropriateness of their content and methods for women and reformulated if necessary. On the other hand, more women-only training schemes are required for the reasons referred to above. Awareness creation and training of trainers, particularly in organizations offering mixed male/female training schemes, are clearly vital elements in efforts to improve existing provisions, as is a conscious attempt to target women in the promotion and marketing of programmes to potential entrepreneurs.

Funding

All member states have public financing schemes to support those going into self-employment or small enterprise creation. In some cases, such as Denmark, Portugal and Belgium, positive take-up by women is recorded, whereas in France and the UK women's use of such programmes is limited. There are, however, very few examples of funding schemes that take particular account of the financial position and requirements of women setting up in business. Limited capital and collateral, projects that start small in terms of capital investment and that are of relatively little commercial interest to traditional financial institutions are common problems (see Kaur and Hayden; Koper this volume). In addition, there is an apparent imbalance between the extent of enterprise funding in favour of larger investments and high-technology or production-related initiatives, and the tertiary sector where many women's enterprise initiatives are concentrated.

Studies have shown that many women starting businesses feel they are subjected to discriminatory attitudes on the part of staff in traditional financial institutions, such as banks (Turner 1989; Koper this volume). They point to the lack of credibility and confidence shown in them, sometimes coupled with demands that collateral be put up by a male family member. Where women's businesses are based on non-traditional enterprise structures or working methods, such as collectives, co-operatives, flexi-time or job-sharing, this tends to act as a further obstacle to securing financial support from conventional funding institutions.

Thus, despite the claims by these institutions that men and women receive equal treatment, in practice, women starting small businesses often come up against obstacles in their attempts to secure financial support from them. Lack of 'required' knowledge and know-how in presentation and negotiating skills, coupled with a lack of self-confidence in some cases, tends to aggravate these obstacles for many women, rendering most conventional financial sources inaccessible to them at business start-up.

In response to these difficulties, financial support programmes specifically addressed to women's enterprise have developed on a limited scale. Examples include the Okobank, founded in Frankfurt in 1988, which offers women initiative loans at a preferential interest rate; Goldrausch in Berlin offers loans and grants to women's enterprises; affiliates of Women's World Banking in France, Italy, and Spain provide guarantee funds for women entrepreneurs seeking loans, as do Stichting Sormentorfonds and Mama Cash in The Netherlands, where women also have access to small business loans through Fonds BV. In France, Portugal, Spain, and Greece certain women have access to grants above the standard rate from the public self-employment/business creation schemes.

However, the only member state in which a public financial assistance scheme specifically directed at women's enterprise exists is France. Launched in 1989, the fund operates by guaranteeing loans made to women's businesses by banks, up to 65 per cent in the case of credit for start-up and 50 per cent of business development loans. Beyond the direct financial benefits of the scheme to a limited number of women's enterprises, the programme furnishes women entrepreneurs with information and guidance, facilitating their access to other forms of support such as training, technical assistance, and consultancy. The scheme has stimulated support for women's enterprise initiatives from local and regional equality officers who are involved in promoting it, and thus provides an important resource point for women entrepreneurs at local level.

In the Community as a whole, financial support suited to the needs of women creating enterprises is clearly fragmentary and inadequate. In an effort to improve the situation, awareness creation and training are key elements. Training for women, to arm them with the basic business and personal skills needed to approach banks and market themselves and their business ventures effectively, is one part of this. The other is awareness creation and training among key staff members in financial institutions to break down discriminatory attitudes towards women starting small businesses. Seminars and meetings that bring the two parties together is a practical means of two-way awareness raising and training.

Rigorous research, monitoring, and evaluation of the appropriateness to new women entrepreneurs of existing schemes and terms of business financing are essential to the preparation of guidelines for action, such that equal opportunities in access to funding sources for enterprise creation becomes a reality.

Networks

In recent years, women entrepreneurs have been joining together through networks and mutual support groups, to meet both social and business goals. Those include the 'Network' of women's enterprises in Ireland, Women in Enterprise in the UK, Terziario Donna in Italy, International Federations of Business and Professional Women, and Associations of Women Heads of Enterprise. Such groups can play an important role in spreading confidence, knowledge and know-how among women entrepreneurs, through exchange of information and experiences and the organization of common projects, such as seminars, meetings, and the 'fostering' of new women entrepreneurs by those with experience – of which 'Mentorscoop', founded in the Netherlands, is an example.

Equally encouraging are initiatives linking support agencies for women entrepreneurs, such as the Women Insurance and Finance Experts Network for women in Germany, the Women Business Advisers Network in Scotland, Association for the Development of Women's Economic Initiatives (ADIEF) which links women in high administrative and executive positions in France, with the aim of lobbying for improved support for women in enterprise. The work of ADIEF was a forerunner to the French government loan guarantee fund for women's enterprise. These networking initiatives, by and for women, are examples of the way women are helping each other to help themselves in the field of entrepreneurship.

EC PROGRAMME FOR WOMEN'S EMPLOYMENT INITIATIVES (LEI-ILE)

Support for employment initiatives, i.e. the setting up of small businesses and not-for-profit ventures, as a means of creating employment, has been part of Community policy since 1984 (Council Resolution OY84C/No 161/01). Because women suffer more acutely from unemployment than men in most member States, an additional specific resolution was taken to combat unemployment among women, which states, inter alia, that local employment initiatives 'offer women worthwhile employment prospects and working conditions' (Council Resolution OY84C/No 161/02).

This EC policy is thus rooted in the recognition of the role of small business creation in combating unemployment, but also in raising the quality of conditions of work for women in promoting the spirit of entrepreneurship and in facilitating their combination of family and professional life. The fundamental aim of the support programme has been to assist women in their efforts to create viable enterprises that provide stable jobs for women at local level. Priority has been given to women who face particular difficulties in gaining access to the labour market, such as the long-term unemployed, those returning to work after a career break, those with limited or outdated skills, young qualified unemployed women, migrants, lone mothers, and disabled women.

Although the Equal Opportunities Unit, DG V of the EC Commission has shown support for women's enterprise since 1983, through the award of small sums to women wishing to create a co-operative or other small business, 1987 saw the launch of a dynamic and broader support programme for women's enterprise/employment initiatives, in the context of the Medium-Term Community Programme for Equal Opportunities (1986-90).

Beyond a series of studies on women's enterprise creation (Turner 1989; Halpern and Szurek 1989), the backbone of this support programme has been aid in funding the start-up costs of women's businesses and technical support, offered to women's enterprises through a network of experts/support agents active throughout the member states of the Community.

Funding

In recognition of the difficulties faced by many women in securing adequate funds for enterprise creation, small grants of 1500-7500 Ecu are awarded to women setting up small businesses throughout the Community. Application has to be made prior to business start-up and the conditions to be met are the creation of at least two full-time jobs (or the part-time equivalent) at start-up, that women manage the enterprise and hold the majority of jobs.

By the end of 1990, some 700 women's businesses throughout the Community were approved for funding with start-up grants from the EC Commission. It is interesting to note the particular take-up of the grant in 'peripheral' areas of the Community: Greece, Portugal, Spain, Ireland, and parts of France. In Portugal and Spain the EC grant acted as a useful complement to other funds secured from the public purse, while in Greece high demand for the EC grant was related more to the paucity of such funding at national level.

Although the amount of funding (up to 7500 Ecu) awarded to each business is small in comparison to the real start-up costs, evaluation meetings with funded enterprises in five member states in 1989/90 indicated that the grant had nevertheless had positive effects on the development of these businesses, directly or indirectly. In some cases, such as Greece and Portugal, the amount in itself represented a significant financial contribution, while in France and Spain, the funding was more important as a lever for securing further support and credibility.

In general, it is felt that the grant confers credibility on the enterprises, facilitating their access to financial support from other sources and raising their professional profile in business and social circles. It has also acted as a positive public relations element in marketing the business to potential clients and has acted as moral encouragement to other local women planning to set up a business.

Lessons for future action have been drawn from evaluation of the weaknesses of the programme, identified during the second EC action programme for equal opportunities (1986-90). It was found that the economic and social goals of the programme, which were to support the development of viable businesses by women in disadvantaged circumstances with the greatest need for all forms of support (training, consultancy, marketing), were not always easily combined. In practice, it was hard to reach this target group, since these are the very women who have least access to information.

This reconfirmed the need for enterprise support initiatives that target these women with information, counselling, advice, and training, at local/regional level, such that they can gain access to funding and make effective use of it. In recognition of this need, in the context of its third Programme for Equal Opportunities (1991-5), the EC Commission Network for Women's LEIs is channelling 'software' support to projects for women's enterprise initiatives, in the areas of pre-training, business training, advice, and information.

Technical support

In January 1987, the EC Commission launched the European Network for Women in Local Employment Initiatives (LEIs), made up of experts working with women starting small businesses in all twelve member states. The essential purpose of the Network is to act as a two-way communication link between the Commission and women taking enterprise initiatives in the Community, and also to provide practical and coordinated support to these women within each member state.

The LEI Network has four key areas of action:

1 Development of the professional and personal capacity of women setting up enterprises and other employment initiatives, particularly through the development of practical tools, transnational in application, on special themes such as: marketing strategies, innovation in support and the training of trainers. The Network will produce the first of a series of Manuals in Autumn 1992, focusing on marketing strategies for trade and co-operation in the Europe of 1993.
2 Exchange of experience and good practice in support of women's enterprise initiatives throughout the Community, through the development of good practice guides, evaluation mechanisms and criteria.
3 Promotion and development of partnerships with relevant programmes and structures, at local/regional, national and Community levels. Already the Network has developed links and proposals for actions in favour of women's enterprise initiatives, with CEDEFOP, DG XXIII and DG V Programmes.
4 EC Commission grants to women's LEIs: the Network plays a key role in the development and effectiveness of this grant scheme, through information dissemination and promotion, guidance and specialist advice to women creating enterprises, evaluation and follow-up of initiatives.

CONCLUSIONS

Business creation is by no means an easy option. Many women, particularly those lacking appropriate training, traditions or experience, face obstacles greater than they imagined in their entrepreneurial development process. These include lack of self-confidence, lack of business contacts and recourse to an enterprise tradition, pressing family responsibilities, limited financial resources, an aversion to risk. Existing enterprise support provisions are largely inadequate or inappropriate to help women help themselves overcome these obstacles.

Rigorous research, monitoring, and evaluation is required, not only of the appropriateness of mixed-sex entrepreneurial support structures but also of women-only schemes. We need to evaluate their particular experiences, and the nature of their contribution to the development of female entrepreneurship and to the achievement of both economic and social goals set by the women themselves.

The past decade has witnessed an increase in enterprise creation among women across the Community, either as an attractive option conferring independence, creativity and the opportunity for personal development that salaried employment seldom offers, or as a sole solution to the problem of unemployment. A new entrepreneurial culture is developing, based on the values and strengths of women, such as creativity, flexibility, an openness to co-operation, a human approach to business relations, attention to social and cultural as well as financial goals in business.

The way forward is thus a two-way process. On the one hand, this way forward is through the development of financial, pre-training, enterprise training, and business support services that are appropriate to the needs of women setting up enterprises, which enable them to meet the challenge of the single market. This means both remodelling many existing mixed-sex entrepreneurial support services and the development of women-only provisions.

On the other hand, these mechanisms should themselves act as levers for change in the opposite direction. That is to say, to a change in the very nature of what is today an essentially male enterprise culture, through its enrichment with the values, visions, and experiences of women.

The Self-Employed Women's Association (SEWA) in India has a saying:

> The Work of a Woman
> is like a vein of
> water flowing
> underground,
> secretly making
> the ground greener

And as Peter Drucker (1977) has observed, 'the making of a different tomorrow is a major responsibility of the managers of today'. It is perhaps in the world of entrepreneurship that the recognition and value of women's contribution is most vital to the making of a better tomorrow in Europe.

11 Female business ownership
Current research and possibilities for the future

Sara Carter

The small business sector has expanded in recent decades, stimulated by changes in the industrial structure of Britain and Government commitment to encourage new forms of economic enterprise. There has been an increased confidence in the potential of small firms to contribute to the regeneration of the British economy (Williams 1985). The importance of small firms has been recognized by Government to the extent that it is now regarded as a vital element to increase the rate of job creation and reorientate social attitudes towards enterprise and entrepreneurship (Weiner 1981). There has been a rise in the rate of new firm formation in the past few years (Ganguly 1985), to the extent that Britain had in the mid 1980s the largest proportion of self-employed people since the 1920s: one-tenth of the working population (Curran 1986).

A substantial part of this increase has been fuelled by the number of women starting businesses. Estimates of the number of self-employed men and women in the United Kingdom display a 'sharply upward trend which has accelerated in the 1980s' (Curran 1986: 3). Between 1981 and 1987 male self-employment had increased by 30 per cent; the number of self-employed women, however, increased by 70 per cent (Department of Employment 1988a). While it is widely accepted that in Britain women now account for 25 per cent of all self-employed, this masks the fact that women actually account for only 16 per cent of all full-time, but more than 70 per cent of all part-time self-employed (Department of Employment 1988a). Similar trends have been noted in other developed countries (van der Wees and Romijn 1987). The United States Small Business Administration reported in 1985 that over the previous decade the number of female business owners grew by 74 per cent, accounting for 37 per cent of all new enterprises. Accordingly, business receipts from female-owned businesses increased from $44 billion to $53 billion in 1983 alone. Women still, however, represent only a minority of entrepreneurs in proportions which vary from one country to another (see Turner this volume). The growth of the small firm sector has led to an associated development of academic research into the small business and the nature of entrepreneurship (Carter et al. 1989; Curran 1986). While many significant studies have been undertaken looking at small firms from economic, business and sociological perspectives, the bulk of the work to date has, *de facto*, concentrated upon the male-owned enterprise. Research into female entrepreneurship and the role of women as proprietors and employers has, until comparatively recently, been largely neglected as an area of serious academic study (Goffee and Scase 1985) despite the fact that greater numbers of women are now choosing self-employment (Curran 1986). Towards the end of the 1980s, however, there was the start of a new research interest into the female-owned enterprise, reflecting both the rise in the number of women starting in business and also increasing academic interest in small business and the nature of entrepreneurship.

Influenced by the existing small business and entrepreneurship literature, early studies of female entrepreneurship concentrated mainly upon the motivations for business start-up (Schreier 1973; Schwartz 1976; Hisrich and Brush 1983; Goffee and Scase 1985) and, to a lesser extent, the gender-related barriers experienced during this phase of business ownership (Hisrich and Brush 1984; Watkins and Watkins 1984; Carter and Cannon 1988b). In Britain, researchers have tried to establish linkages between motivations for female self-employment and the overall position of women in the labour market (Goffee and Scase 1985; Cromie and Hayes 1988; Carter and Cannon 1988b). Few of the studies of female entrepreneurs have developed sophisticated taxonomies, preferring to identify female proprietors as an homogenous group, and until recently there has been an implicit acceptance by researchers that – beyond the start-up phase – few significant differences exist between male and female owned and managed companies (see Johnson and Storey this volume). Scholars of small business have noted that our cumulative knowledge of female entrepreneurship remains limited (Curran 1986; Stevenson 1983), generally lacks utility and rigour (Soloman and Fernald 1988; Allen and Truman 1988) and presents a static and therefore distorted view of the process of female business ownership (Carter and Cannon 1988b).

NORTH AMERICAN RESEARCH

There has been more interest and research into the nature and experience of the female entrepreneur in North America than in Britain. Early, influential studies of female entrepreneurs (where 'entrepreneur' is used as a synonym for owner-manager) tended to describe their motives for starting a business (Schreier 1973), their personality characteristics (Lavoie 1987), and the problems they encountered (Collom 1981; Hisrich and Brush 1986).

Schreier's (1973) study of female entrepreneurs demonstrated that the female entrepreneur had much in common with her male counterpart, with the exception of the types of business owned by women. Businesses owned by women tended to reflect traditional female employment in the labour market, mainly in the service sectors. Schwartz (1976) also found a predominance of service-based businesses. Schwartz concluded that female motivations for business start-up were similar to those of men, that is, the search for independence and the challenge of business ownership. The greatest barriers to their business success, however, were financial discrimination, lack of training and business knowledge, and underestimating the cost of sustaining a business.

Hisrich and Brush (1983) concentrated on motivations for business start-up and examined the demographic characteristics of female entrepreneurs. Motivations for business start-up were described as job satisfaction, independence, and achievement. Major problems faced by women tended to be under-capitalization, and the lack of experience, knowledge, and training necessary for business ownership. Many respondents reported difficulties in 'overcoming some of the social beliefs that women are not as serious as men about business'. Hisrich and Brush found evidence of the contrasting experience of women operating in different sectors. Women in non-traditional female sectors (that is, those dominated by male employees, such as construction and manufacturing industries) experienced more problems in raising finance. In both non-traditional and new sectors, female business owners were hampered by their lack of business training. Hisrich and Brush (1983) concluded that barriers experienced by female entrepreneurs often relate to the sectors in which they trade. A later study (Hisrich and Brush 1986) focused on different types of female-owned business and confirmed the lack of support offered to female proprietors in non-traditional sectors.

In a study of 183 female-owned businesses in Canada, it was found that a number of barriers faced female business-owners. These

Female business ownership 151

included a lack of confidence, intimidation, lack of credibility, and a lack of peer support (Stevenson 1983). Many interviewees experienced a sense of guilt (or role conflict) due to difficulties in meeting both business and family commitments. Such experiences have also been reported in Britain (Goffee et al. 1982; Goffee and Scase 1985; Carter and Cannon 1988b).

BRITISH RESEARCH

In Britain, studies specifically investigating female entrepreneurship have been scarce in comparison with the volume of work undertaken in the area of small business and entrepreneurship. As with other research into social phenomena, gender effects have frequently been omitted from 'mainstream' studies. It has been noted that historically women have been left off the small business research agenda or made invisible by research practices or in other ways written out of the analysis of self-employment (Hamilton 1990). Hamilton cites an example of how this is done (1990: 6–7). Rees and Shah 'exclude a number of categories of people and then a whole gender ". . . in order to obtain sharper results" '(1986: 101). Among the excluded are 'those who are not heads of their households (mainly women); those who worked for less than thirty hours a week (mainly women); females (on the basis that "self-employment is predominantly a male preserve")' (Rees and Shah (1986: 101). Hamilton states that

> this single example serves as a clear statement of androcentrism. Androcentrism allows for the 'elevation of the masculine to the level of the universal and the ideal, it is the honoring of men and the male principal above women and the female. This perception creates a belief in male superiority and a value system in which female values, experiences and behaviours are viewed as inferior' (Shakeshaft and Nowell 1984: 187–88).
>
> (Hamilton 1990: 7)

The elevation of the masculine to this level is, as Hamilton points out, 'to create a blind spot on the researcher's lens' (1990: 7).

The interest in women and small business ownership as a research topic in its own right has occurred mainly because 'a degree of solidarism has taken place through the actions and deliberations of (female scholars) who through a feminist analysis of the social construction of women's position in society have been able to expose the subjective nature of male cultural domination' (Hamilton 1990: 6). Nevertheless, as Curran comments:

152 *Women in business*

to date there have been only two influential (British) studies (Watkins and Watkins 1984 and Goffee and Scase 1985) plus a more recent study of female aspiring small business owners (Cromie 1984). All have been relatively small-scale – involving samples of fifty or less – and all have had problems in constructing what might be seen as a properly representative sample for the usual reason of a lack of adequate sampling frames.

(Curran 1986:20)

Using a sample comparing fifty-eight women and forty-three male business owners Watkins and Watkins (1984) found that the backgrounds and experiences of women differed significantly from those of men. Men were more likely to have work experience which was related to their present venture. Self-employment provided them with an essentially similar occupation with the added attraction of autonomy. The study also found that most women were unprepared for business start-up and consequently could be seen to take greater risks than their male counterparts. Women often had no relevant experience which facilitated their entry into non-traditional areas. The authors concluded that this lack of prior experience affects the choice of sectors in which women are capable of establishing viable businesses, forcing them into traditionally female sectors. Moreover, in traditional sectors, successful female entrepreneurs act as role models, helping other women to confront and overcome problems. Choice of business sector was determined by consideration of which areas posed the least obstacles to their success. These were perceived to be those where technical and financial barriers to business entry were low and where managerial proficiency was not essential to success. As Watkins and Watkins emphasize: 'choice is determined by high motivation to immediate independence tempered by economic rationality, rather than by a conscious desire to operate "female-type" businesses' (1984: 230).

Goffee and Scase (1985) identified a typology of female entrepreneurs, based on two factors. First, their relative attachment to *conventional* entrepreneurial ideals in the form of individualism and self-reliance. Second, the willingness of the female entrepreneur to accept conventional gender roles, often subordinate to men. (A similar profile of the female entrepreneur was described by Cromie and Hayes 1988.) The typology consisted of four 'types' of women: *conventional* entrepreneurs, committed to both entrepreneurial ideals and conventional gender roles; *innovative* entrepreneurs, who held a strong belief in entrepreneurial ideals but had a relatively low attachment to conventional gender roles; *domestic* entrepreneurs, who believed in conventional female roles and held low attachment to entrepreneurial ideals; and finally, *radical* entrepreneurs who held low attachment to both, often organizing their businesses on a political collectivist basis. This typology has been criticized on a number of levels. Allen and Truman (1988) argue that the two factors upon which the typology is based, that is, entrepreneurial ideals and adherence to conventional gender roles, are not appropriate for the analysis of female entrepreneurial behaviour. They state that the socio-economic reality of women's lives means that the majority have very little choice over how attached they can be to 'entrepreneurial ideals':

> For example, 'self-help and personal responsibility and reliance' have different connotations in different contexts. A single parent trying to earn an income for her family may indeed demonstrate 'entrepreneurial ideals' but the outcome of her entrepreneurship would be quite different from that of a single, childless, male entrepreneur.
>
> (Allen and Truman 1988: 9)

Allen and Truman's criticism of the second factor identified by Goffee and Scase (1985), 'conventionally defined gender roles or the extent to which women accept their subordination to men', centres around the fact that:

> an immediate problem with this approach is that it implies an homogenous experience of women's subordination by men. There is ample evidence in published literature to suggest that female subordination differs in relation to social class, ethnic origin, marital status as well as numerous other factors, both structural and personal.
>
> (Allen and Truman 1988: 9)

Other researchers point out that while the Goffee and Scase typology highlights the often overlooked fact that female entrepreneurs are not a homogeneous group, it perhaps underestimates two important features of business ownership (Carter and Cannon 1988b). First, business ownership, especially in the small firms sector, is a dynamic and often turbulent process, businesses expand, contract, and diversify. Owner-managers may seek to stabilize their businesses, but firms rarely exist in the same form for long. While small firms often remain small, diversity exists within these limits. Thus, cottage industries can become stable thriving firms; self-employed designers can become manufacturers; and manufacturers can diversify to produce specialized products. Second, the typology underestimates the effect business ownership has on the individual entrepreneur, many of whom change with experience. Thus, the 'domestic' entrepreneurs may, by the very experience of business ownership, become dedicated business owners with a very strong attachment to entrepreneurial ideals.

Many of the problems inherent in research into this area stem from the lack of adequate sampling frames. The lack of nationally collected data detailing information on female entrepreneurs makes the construction of a representative sample impossible. Most studies of female owner-managers (as with studies with no gender focus) have used small samples constructed according to the particular interests of the researchers (Curran 1986). Goffee and Scase, for example, employed a sample of fifty-four women 'from home-based, self-employed proprietors to owner-managers of international enterprises' (Goffee and Scase 1985: 39). Their sample, however, was skewed towards those sectors in which women traditionally participate and confined to a particular geographical region (the South-East of England).

A British study constructed a sample more closely related to the profile of female self-employed and owner-managers as suggested by the General Household Survey analysed by Curran (1986) (Carter and Cannon 1988b). Carter and Cannon (1988b) found that the motivations for female business start-up were found to replicate superficially those of male entrepreneurs. However, while the 'search for independence' was the most cited reason for start-up, this study emphasized that a single notion of independence masked the complexities of the issue. Women at different stages of their lives define independence differently, usually depending upon their background, age, and experience. While some women felt that business ownership would free them from the perceived confines of the formal labour market and gender related career blocks, others used proprietorship as a means of returning to the labour market after a period devoted to motherhood.

Carter and Cannon found that broadly the same operational problems are faced by all business owners and it is difficult to establish the extent to which these problems are exacerbated by gender (1988b). Certain specific areas of business ownership were perceived by the respondents as being gender related: late payment of bills; a tendency to undercharge; getting business and finding clients; and finally, the effect of proprietorship upon personal and domestic circumstances. The effects of these operational problems and the strategies used to overcome them varied between firms. Women running businesses with only a small capital base were less able to cope with late payments.

Lack of assertiveness in collecting debts was perceived by some respondents as a gender related problem. Similarly, while price cutting was used by many proprietors as a market entry strategy, for many respondents undercharging often reflected a lack of confidence in both their products and their business skills (see also Jones this volume).

Difficulties in accessing start-up capital, coupled with delayed payments and undercharging had an inevitable impact on many companies. Few of the newer businesses in the sample were able to achieve the growth desired by the proprietor within the first two years. Older businesses, most of which invested heavily at start-up, demonstrated an ability to access ongoing and growth capital and a subsequently greater rate of growth. It appeared, therefore, that once obstacles regarding finance had been overcome, usually at start-up, female proprietors had few problems with recurrent finance. The barriers seemed to occur at certain key transitional stages; the move from part-time to full-time working, the start-up, and the move to a new market requiring large capital inputs.

Employee relations were perceived as posing the most difficult and intractable of all problems. Even respondents with management experience in larger companies felt a need to learn new skills. Older women often successfully used an overtly matriarchal style, characterized by a unitaristic view of employee relations (see Vokins this volume). Younger women, inexperienced in management and lacking the age to develop a credible management style, struggled most. Some suggested that male employees were unwilling to accept female employers and dealt with this by channelling requests through a male manager or superviser. One respondent referred to an 'assumed competence' which tends to be attributed to most men but not to most women. As in the studies by Stevenson (1983) and Hisrich and Brush (1984, 1986) many respondents in our research stated that they had to earn credibility, not just with their business colleagues and customers, but also with their employees. Most women felt strongly that many of the problems of credibility were gender related.

Many interviewees stated that they were not feminists and, moreover, appeared hostile to that philosophy. In contrast, a significant minority (40 per cent) did believe that aspects of business ownership were harder for women, often despite their inability to identify specific areas in which discrimination exists. The lack of any previous opportunity to develop business skills and knowledge was often given as the key difference between male and female business owners.

As we have seen from the discussion above, it is clear that some contemporary research is beginning to demonstrate that women do have different experiences of entrepreneurship from their male counterparts. Research into female entrepreneurship in Britain suggests that the motivations of women starting in business differ from their male counterparts and also provide some insight into gender-related inequalities experienced by women starting in business. The results suggest that it is more difficult for women to start in business and that, once trading, they face problems which may inhibit company growth. What is also clear is that the issue of female entrepreneurship is of growing importance, if only from a quantitative perspective. As we saw earlier, in both Great Britain and the United States of America, the rate of increase in self-employment has been greater for women than men (Department of Employment 1988a; Small Business Administration 1985). This increase is mirrored in other countries. An ILO report stated that:

> an estimated 35 per cent of all households worldwide are headed by women, women show everywhere an increasing labour force participation but are at the same time harder hit by unemployment, [and] levels of poverty force large numbers of women to pursue survival strategies in the informal sector, including self-employment and micro-enterprise development.
> (van der Wees and Romijn 1987: 2)

METHODOLOGICAL PROBLEMS

So far in this chapter an overview has been given of research into female entrepreneurship. This has addressed issues of motivation, barriers to entry, and gender related problems, and has generally provided a description of female-owned businesses in particular countries. But despite the increasing interest in this area and the advances made in our understanding of female entrepreneurship, certain aspects of both the research techniques used and the current research agenda have impeded further progress. Three problem areas appear to be of immediate importance and expose the field to substantial external criticism. First, current research has depended upon small scale sample sizes, often involving samples of fifty or less. The second, related problem has been the propensity of researchers to adopt qualitative data collection techniques. Lastly, with very few exceptions, researchers have tended to study the phenomena of female entrepreneurship in isolation, that is without reference to a broader theoretical framework. Arguably, these problems will have to be addressed before this field of study can develop further.

Sample sizes

First we address the problem of sample size. As we have seen, many of the studies conducted in both the United States and Britain have employed similar techniques, similar sample sizes, taken a similar focus and, perhaps as a consequence, yielded similar results. Thus, there is a serious risk that the existing research, although useful in providing 'colour', has been blighted by a lack of systematic endeavour. We have already seen that one critic of the field has, quite correctly, pointed out that small samples have been a major stumbling block in our knowledge acquisition (Curran 1986). To an extent, this criticism could equally be applied to many 'mainstream' studies of small business ownership and entrepreneurship, which do not take a gender focus.

The problem of small scale sampling occurs partly because there is a serious shortfall in research funding in the social sciences generally. Faced with a normal academic requirement to undertake research and a shortage of available funding with which to fulfill their duties, scholars often have little choice but to compile samples from local sources. Such measures inevitably lead them to employ small scale, geographically biased samples. Another reason for the lack of adequate sampling frames is that gender as a variable is often omitted from large scale national research projects into the small business community. While many studies are undertaken annually into issues which affect small business owners, many of which include female entrepreneurs, the subsequent analysis does not often use gender as a variable. Thus, while national information has been gathered from female business owners, researchers specializing in this area cannot access the data. As a consequence there is no national profile of the female entrepreneur, and gender specific studies are bound to be biased.

The increasing interest in this subject area is beginning to resolve both of these issues. Greater and more widespread interest in female business ownership from within the academic community, and also from the wider public and media, has been a contributory factor in attracting new research funding. The increased funding available, particularly from government and quasi-government sources, has focused attention on the possible gender dimension in national studies of small business and entrepreneurship. In the future, more sophisticated sampling techniques will be demanded if studies are to have the same influence as that generated by the earlier pioneering work. It is likely that small scale sampling in research on female entrepreneurship will become an issue from the past.

Data collection

In seeking to improve the quality of contemporary gender based research, the second issue to be addressed is the emphasis upon qualitative research techniques. It is, of course, inevitable that a shortage of research funding, coupled with inadequate sample frameworks, will lead scholars to adopt qualitative techniques, in particular personal interviews, as their favoured research tool. There are, however, certain inherent problems with this method. Researchers generally face methodological problems when relying upon verbal reports and individual explanations to investigate previous or current experiences. Not only are there problems concerning the accuracy of retrospective recall, there are, especially in the area of gender based research, also difficulties in distinguishing 'perceived' problems from 'real' problems. Much research in the field of female entrepreneurship has depended upon personal interviewing techniques as a primary source of data collection. However, it could be surmised that the social and political background of the interviewees often determines whether discrimination, which is the central issue, is perceived and recognized as such. In other instances, it could be seen that the interview itself is a determining factor. By probing and encouraging interviewees to describe their experiences in terms of gender related issues, the interviewer may raise the level of consciousness and recognition of gender discrimination. Where discrimination is recognized by respondents, it is generally a function of two factors: first, the general awareness of the constraints on labour force participation of female employees in the overall economy and second, direct experience of gender discrimination as a self-employed woman. In a personal interview it is exceptionally difficult to separate the two factors. Although impossible to isolate and address quantitatively, the issue of perception versus reality is central to many of the findings of studies of female entrepreneurship, particularly in the attribution of certain business problems to gender related barriers. This can be seen as a direct result of the use of personal interviewing techniques.

There are, however, good reasons why researchers should use personal interviews and other qualitative techniques for gender based research (Bernard 1973; Scott 1985). Scholars have consistently demonstrated that it is exceptionally difficult to extract experiences of gender discrimination via the use of quantitative techniques. If qualitative techniques are to remain as the favoured method, then researchers must be prepared to improve the methods they use. This can be achieved by learning from the methodological debates, particularly in sociology, which have been conducted over the past decade (Roberts 1981) and by increasing sample sizes from the norm of fifty and ensuring that the research in the field can withstand the most rigourous external scrutiny. Nevertheless, our knowledge cannot progress simply by using these methods alone. Researchers must also be prepared to employ large scale samples and data collected quantitatively. Secondary sources also offer great promise. There are several rich and, as yet, largely unexplored sources of secondary data, such as the Labour Force Survey and the General Household Survey, which could be utilized to further our knowledge of female entrepreneurship.

Theoretical approaches

The third major problem has been the propensity of researchers to study female entrepreneurship in isolation, without a suitable academic context or larger theoretical framework. It has been noted that this has been an unfortunate feature of much small business research generally (Cannon et al. 1986; Curran 1986) and this cannot be applied solely to research studies with a specific gender focus. Nevertheless, there have been signs that the broader field of small business research is maturing and that the theoretical issues are emerging. This has been brought about by two decades of sustained research interest culminating in a British national research initiative funded by the Economic and Social Research Council. However, the more specific area of female entrepreneurship needs to develop in the same way.

The lack of an academic or theoretical context can be seen to be a direct result of the fact that the study of female entrepreneurship, as with small business research generally, does not fit neatly into any established academic discipline. As such, the research effort has to cross traditional discipline boundaries. To date, much of the existing research effort has been undertaken by scholars from Management Sciences, but there has been little sign that the subject has progressed much over the past ten years, in terms of content, focus or rigour, or even that knowledge has been cumulative. Arguably, these problems can only be resolved when researchers of female entrepreneurship start to build a theoretical core from a number of disciplinary sources. Disciplines such as sociology and social psychology can play an important role here. While 'mainstream' small business researchers have learnt to draw from the knowledge, experience, and literature of many disciplines, the field of female entrepreneurship has yet to mature in this manner. Although the linkages between research into self-employment per se and the overall labour market have been made by numerous researchers (Scase and Goffee 1982; Curran et al. 1986; Curran and Burrows 1988b), the linkages between female self-employment and the position of women in the labour market have not always been clearly established. Scholars investigating female entrepreneurship must not only be able to draw from an array of disciplinary sources, they must also learn to place their findings within the broader context as well (see Allen and Truman 1992, for further discussion).

CONCLUSION

There are signs that the study of female entrepreneurship is developing and maturing. Interest in the topic, which has evolved over the past decade, is continuing to grow and it is expected that this new phenomenon will attract more interest from a number of established academic disciplines. In particular, the contribution of sociologists and social psychologists is beginning to have a positive impact on the quality of research being undertaken. The late 1980s witnessed an increase in the quantity and quality of research funding available for the study of small business research generally. Our knowledge of women proprietors, their motivations, experiences, management styles and abilities will undoubtedly benefit from this. In addition, there are signs that new research is beginning to build on previous work rather than simply confirming it. The process of research review has started, and with that methodologies and techniques will be changed and strengthened to accommodate more rigorous scrutiny. In terms of research on female business ownership, the possibilities for the future are many and the outlook is good.

Bibliography

Ahmed, A.S. and Ahmed, Z. (1981) ' "Mor and Tor": Binary and opposing models of pukthun womanhood', in T. S. Epstein and R. A. Watts (eds) *The Endless Day*, Oxford: Pergamon Press.
Allen, S. (1982) 'Gender inequality and class formation', in A. Giddens and G. Mackenzie (eds) *Social Class and the Division of Labour: Essays in Honour of Ilya Neustadt*, Cambridge: Cambridge University Press.
—— (1989) 'Economic recession and gender divisions in western capitalism', in Richard Scase (ed.) *Industrial Societies: Crisis and Division in Western Capitalism and State Socialism*, London: George Allen and Unwin.
Allen, S. and Truman, C. (1988) 'Women's work and success in women's businesses', paper presented to the 11th National Small Firms Policy and Research Conference, Cardiff.
—— (1992) 'Women, business and self-employment: a conceptual minefield', in S. Arber and N. Gilbert (eds) *Women and Working Lives: Divisions and Change*, London: Macmillan.
Allen, S., Truman, C. and Wolkowitz, C. (1992) 'Home-based work: self-employment and small business', in P. Leighton and A. Felstead (eds) *The New Entrepreneurs: Self-Employment and Small Business in Europe*, London: Kogan Page.
Allen, S. and Wolkowitz, C. (1987) *Homeworking – Myths and Realities*, London: Macmillan.
Amsterdam–Rotterdam Bank (AMRO) (1988) *Faal-en slaagfactoren van startende ondernemingen'* Amsterdam: AMRO.
Andersen, V. (1989) 'A comparative study of potential female entrepreneurs in Denmark and Scotland', unpublished MBA dissertation, University of Edinburgh.
Atkinson, J. (1984a) 'Manpower strategies for flexible organisations', *Personnel Management*, August.
—— (1984b) *Flexibility, Uncertainty and Manpower Management*, Report No. 89, Brighton: Institute of Manpower Studies.
Bangun, M. (1985) 'Family-rooted productive activities', unpublished Ph.D. thesis, University of Indonesia, Jakarta.
Barron, K.J. and Norris, G.M. (1976) 'Sexual divisions and the dual labour market', in D. Barker and S. Allen (eds) *Dependence and Exploitation in Work and Marriage*, London: Longman.

Bernard, J. (1973) 'My four revolutions: an autobiographical history of the American Sociological Association', *American Journal of Sociology* 78: 773-91.
Birmingham Women's Enterprise Development Agency (1990) Unpublished Research Report
Boulgarides, J.D. (1984) 'Comparison of male and female business managers', *Leadership and Organisational Development* 5: Part 5.
Boyer, R. (1987) 'Labour flexibilities: many forms, uncertain effects', *Labour And Society* 12, 1: 107-29.
—— (ed.) (1988) *The Search for Labour Market Flexibility: The European Economies In Transition*, Oxford: Clarendon Press.
Broadley, C.J. (1990) 'Factors which influence potential entrepreneurs in their decision whether or not to start-up a business: a case study of women going into business', unpublished BA dissertation, University of Stirling.
Bromley, R. and Gerry, C. (eds) (1979) *Casual Work and Poverty in Third World Cities*, Chichester: John Wiley & Sons.
Brown, P. and Scase, R. (eds) (1991) *Poor Work*, Milton Keynes: Open University Press.
Burke, W.W. (1979) 'Leaders and their development', *Group and Organisational Studies* 1: Part 3, September.
Burr, R. (1986) *Female Tycoons: Interviews with 12 Top Business Women*, London: Rosters Ltd.
Burrows, R. and Curran, J. (1991) 'Not such a small business: reflections on the rhetoric, the reality and the future of the enterprise culture', in M. Cross and G. Payne (eds) *Work and the Enterprise Culture*, London: The Falmer Press.
Business in the Community (BIC) (1989) *A Review of the Enterprise Agency Network*, London: Business in the Community.
Cannon, T., Carter, S. Nenadic, S. and Faulkner, W. (1986) 'Research in small business', unpublished Report to the Economic and Social Research Council, Industry and Employment Committee.
Cannon, T., Carter, S., Rosa, P., Baddon, L. and McClure, R. (1988) *Female Entrepreneurs*, Report to Department of Employment and Shell UK Ltd, University of Stirling: Scottish Enterprise Foundation.
Careers Research and Advisory Centre (1986) *Enterprise - A Learning Culture?* Reflections and Workshop. Reports from the Second Education for Enterprise Network Conference, Cambridge: CRAC Conference Office, Bateman Street.
Carr, M. (1984) *Blacksmith, Baker, Roofing-Sheet Maker*, London: Intermediate Technology Publications.
Carter, S. and Cannon, T. (1988a) 'Women in business', *Employment Gazette* 96, 10: 565-71.
—— (1988b) 'Female entrepreneurs, a study of female business owners; their motivations, experiences and strategies for success', *Department of Employment Research Paper*, No.65, London: HMSO.
Carter, S., Cannon, T., Nenadic, S. and Faulkner, W. (1989) 'Research in small business: the nature, the role and the impact of a new research field', in P. Rosa, S. Carter, S. Birley, T. Cannon and K. O'Neill (eds) *The Contribution of Small Business Research*, Aldershot: Gower.

Casey, B. and Creigh, S. (1988) 'Self-employment in Great Britain: its definition in the labour force survey in tax and social security law and in labour law', *Work, Employment and Society* 2(3): 381-91.

Cassidy, R. jnr. (1974) *Exchange by Private Treaty*, Austin: The University of Texas.

Castillo, G.T. (1976) *The Philippino Woman as Manpower, The Image and the Empirical Reality*, Laguna: Los Banos University Press.

Centraal Bureau voor de Statistiek (CBS) (1985) *Arbeidskrachtentelling*, CBS: Den Haag.

Chaganti, R. (1986) 'Management in women-owned enterprises', *Journal of Small Business Management* 24: 18-29, October.

Chan Shui-Ying, L. (1988) *A Strategic Analysis of Current Support Provision for Female Entrepreneurs in Scotland*, unpublished M.Sc. thesis, University of Stirling.

Clutterbuck, D. and Devine, M. (eds) (1987) *Businesswoman, Present and Future*, London: Macmillan.

Collom, D. (1981) 'Canadian women owner managers', report, Ottowa: Ottowa Small Business Secretariat.

Commission of European Communities (1989) 'Employment in Europe', Brussels: DG V.

Cottam, C.M. (1991) 'Purdah magnates: hidden traders in Rajasthan', in C. M. Cottam-Ellis and S. Rao (eds) *Woman, Aid and Development*, Delhi: Hindustan Publishing Corporation.

Creigh, S., Roberts, C., Gorman, A. and Sawyer, P. (1986) 'Self-employment in Britain, results From Labour Force Surveys 1981-1984', *Employment Gazette*, June: 183-94.

Cromie, S. (1984) 'The motivations of aspiring male and female entrepreneurs', paper presented to the 6th National Small Firms Policy and Research Conference, Trent Business School.

Cromie, S. and Hayes, J. (1988) 'Towards a typology of female entrepreneurs', *Sociological Review* 36, 1, February: 87-113.

Cuba, R., De Cenzo, D. and Anish, A. (1983) 'Management practices of successful female business owners', *American Journal of Small Business* VIII 2: 40-6.

Curran, J. (1986) *Bolton Fifteen Years On: A Review and Analysis of Small Business Research in Britain 1971-1986*, London: Small Business Research Trust.

Curran, J. and Burrows, R. (1988a) *Small Business Owners and the Self-Employed in Britain: A Secondary Analysis of the General Household Survey 1979-1984*, End of Grant Report to ESRC, June.

—— (1988b) *Enterprise in Britain: A National Profile of Small Business Owners and the Self-Employed*, London: Small Business Research Trust.

Curran, J. and Stanworth, J. (1989) 'Education and training for enterprise, some problems of classification, evaluation, policy and research', *International Small Business Journal* 7, 2.

Curran, J., Stanworth, J. and Watkins, D. (eds) (1986) *The Survival of the Small Firm* Volumes 1-2, Aldershot: Gower.

Daune-Richard, A.M. (1988) 'Gender relations and female labour: a consideration of sociological categories', in J. Jenson, E. Hagan and C. Reddy (eds) *Feminization of the Labour Force*, Cambridge: Polity Press.

Davidson, M. and Cooper, C. (1983) *Women Managers: Their Problems and What can be done to Help Them*, Sheffield: Manpower Services Commission.
Davies, R. (1979) 'Informal sector or subordinate mode of production? A model', in R. Bromley and C. Gerry (eds) *Casual Work and Poverty in Third World Cities*, Chichester: John Wiley & Sons.
Delamont, S. (1980) *The Sociology of Women*, London: Allen & Unwin.
Department Of Employment (1986) *Building Businesses not Barriers*, Government White Paper, Cmnd 9794, London: HMSO.
—— (1988a) '1987, Labour Force Survey – preliminary results', *Employment Gazette* March: 144–58.
—— (1988b) *Assistance to Small Firms*, Report by the Comptroller at Auditor General, London: HMSO.
—— (1989) *Small firms in Britain*, Central Office of Information, London: HMSO.
—— (1990) 'Women in the Labour Market: Results from the 1989 Labour Force Survey, *Employment Gazette* December: 619–43.
De Rijk, C.G.H. (1987) 'Voorwaarden voor positieve aktie in de arbeidsorganisatie', in *Vrouwen hebben voorrang*, Amsterdam: FNV-centrum ondernemingsraden, Uitgeverij Raamgracht.
Devine, M. and Clutterbuck, D. (1985) 'The rise of the entrepreneur', *Management Today* January: 63–71.
Dhamija, J. (1981) *Women and Handicrafts: Myth and Reality*, New York: Seeds Report No. 4.
Drucker, P. (1977) *Management*, London: Pan Books.
—— (1984) *The Practice of Management*, London: Pan.
EEC (1987) 'Non-salaried working women in Europe: women running their own businesses or working independently – women involved in their husband's professional activity', Brussels: Commission of the EC.
Elson, D. and Pearson, R. (eds) (1989) *Women's Employment and Multinationals in Europe*, Basingstoke: Macmillan Press.
Emler, N. and Abrams, D. (1990) 'The sexual distribution of benefits and burdens in the household: adolescent experiences and expectations', *Social Justice Research* 3: 139–56.
Employment Gazette (1988a) *Questions in Parliament*, 96, 9: 512–13, London: HMSO.
—— (1988b) Small Firms are Job Creators, 96, 11: 585, London: HMSO.
—— (1989) *Historical Supplement* No.2 November 97, 11: 2–59, London: HMSO.
EOC (1988) *Women into Business: Strategies for Change*, Manchester: Equal Opportunities Commission.
Epstein, T. S. (1979) 'An outline for action by WFP', unpublished consultancy report, Rome: World Food Programme.
—— (1982) *Urban Food Marketing and Third World Rural Development*, London: Croom Helm.
Fevre, R. (1986) 'Contract work in the recession', in K. Purcell, S. Wood, A. Waton and S. Allen (eds) *The Changing Experience of Employment: Restructuring and Recession*, Basingstoke: Macmillan.
Food and Agriculture Organization (FAO) (undated) 'Promoting the participation of women in food marketing and credit', unpublished paper, Rome: Marketing and Credit Service.

Galbraith, J. K. (1962) *The Affluent Society*, London: Penguin Books in association with Hamish Hamilton (first published in Great Britain by Hamish Hamilton 1958).

Ganguly, P. (1985) *UK Small Business Statistics and International Comparisons*, London: Harper & Row.

Gerry, C. (1985) The working class and small enterprises in the UK recession', in N. Redclift and E. Mingione (eds) *Beyond Employment*, Oxford: Basil Blackwell.

Gershuny, J.I. (1979) 'The informal economy: its role in industrial society', *Futures*, 11, 1, February: 3-15.

—— (1985) 'Economic development and the change in the mode of provision of services', in N. Redclift and E. Mingione (eds) *Beyond Employment*, Oxford: Basil Blackwell.

Gershuny, J.I. and Pahl, R.E. (1979/80) 'Work outside employment: some preliminary speculations', *New Universities Quarterly*, xxxiv, 1, Winter: 120-35.

Goffee, R. and Scase, R. (1985) *Women in Charge: The Experiences of Female Entrepreneurs*, London: George Allen & Unwin.

—— (1987) *Entrepreneurship in Europe*, Worcester: Croom Helm.

Goffee, R., Scase, R. and Pollack, M. (1982) 'Why some women decide to become their own boss', *New Society*, 9 September: 408-10.

—— (1983) 'Business ownership and women's subordination: a preliminary study of female proprietors', *Sociological Review*, 31: 624-48.

Goldstein, N. (1984) 'The new training initiative: a great leap backward?', *Capital and Class*, 23, Summer: 83-106.

Goldthorpe, J. H. (1980) *Social Mobility and Class Structure in Modern Britain*, Oxford: Clarendon Press.

Government White Paper (1986) 'Building businesses . . . not barriers', Cmnd 9794 HMSO.

Haas, L. and Nesemann, C. (1988) Women's local employment initiatives, Brussels: Commission of the European Communities.

Hakim, C. (1988) 'Self employment in Britain: recent trends and current issues', *Work, Employment and Society* 2, 4: 421-50.

—— (1989) 'New recruits to self-employment in the 1980s', *Employment Gazette* 3, 4: 286-97

Halpern, M. and Szurek, J.C. (1989) 'Business creation by women: motivations, situations and perspectives', Brussels: Commission of the European Communities.

Hamilton, D. (1990) 'An "ecological" basis for the analysis of gender differences in the predisposition to self-employment', Paper presented to the RENT Conference, Cologne.

Hampson, A. (1982) *The Lay Perspective: The Construction of Personality*, London: Routledge & Kegan Paul.

Handy, C. (1985) *Gods of Management*, London: Pan.

Hayden, C. (forthcoming) 'A case study of the clothing industry in the West Midlands', in D. Gillingwater and P. Totterdill (eds) *Prospects for Industrial Policy in the 1990s: The Case of the British Textiles and Clothing Industry*, London: Gower.

Hertz, L. (1986) *Business Amazons*, London: Andre Deutsch.

Hill, P. (1962) 'Some characteristics of indigenous West African enterprise', *Economic Bulletin of the Economic Society of Ghana* VI: 3-14.

Hisrich, R. and Brush, C. (1983) 'The woman entrepreneur: implications of family, education and occupational experience', in *Frontiers of Entrepreneurship Research Proceedings*, Wellesley, Massachusetts: Babson College: 255–70.
—— (1984) 'The woman entrepreneur', *Journal of Small Business Management* 22, 1: 30–7.
—— (1986) *The Woman Entrepreneur*, Lexington, Massachusetts: Lexington Books.
Hobbs, D. (1991) 'Business as a master metaphor: working class entrepreneurship and business-like policing', in R. Burrows (ed) *Deciphering the Enterprise Culture: Entrepreneurship, Petty Capitalism and the Restructuring of Britain*, London: Routledge.
Holmquist, C. and Sundin, E. (1989) 'The growth of women entrepreneurship – push or pull factors?', paper presented at the Third Workshop on recent Research in Entrepreneurship, University of Durham.
Howieson, C. (1988) Women and business creation in Scotland, Edinburgh: CEI: 5.
Hughey, A. and Gelman, E. (1986) 'Managing the women's way: does corporate America need "feminine skills"?', *Newsweek* 17 March: 40–1.
Hunt, A. (ed) (1988) *Women and Paid Work: Issues of Equality*, London: Macmillan.
Hymounts, C. (1986) 'The corporate women – the glass ceiling', *Wall Street Journal*, 24 March.
Iglesias, G.U. (1984) 'Socio-cultural, Legal and Other Factors Affecting Women Entrepreneurs and Managers in the Philippines', unpublished paper, Vienna: UNIDO.
Illo, J.F. (1977) *Involvement by Choice*, Quezon City: Institute of Philippine Culture.
Jenson, J., Hagen, E. and Reddy, C. (eds) (1988) *Feminization of the Labour Force*, Cambridge: Polity Press.
Jones, M. (1990) 'The implications for policy decisions of a study of female entrepreneurs in a rural area over eighteen months', United Kingdom Enterprise Management Research Association, Thirteenth Small Firms Policy and Research Conference, Harrogate.
Josefowitz, N. (1980) *Paths to Power*, Reading, Massachusetts: Addison-Wesley.
Joss, S. (1988) 'Production credit for rural women in Nepal', *Rural Development in Practice*, I, 1: 11–19.
Kaur, D. and Hayden, C. (1990) *Clothing Business Start Up Project*, Birmingham: West Midlands Enterprise Board.
Knight, G. and Taylor, A. (1985) *Economic Roles of Women in the Caribbean, with Particular Reference to Higgler Women*, prepared for UNESCO Jamaica: Urban Development Corporation.
Koopman, A.C. and Walvis, C. (1986) *Vrouwen zelfstandig, perspectieven op het ondernemerschap*, Den Haag: Emancipatieraad.
Koper, G. and Vermunt, R. (1988) *Vrouwen en bedrijfskredietverlening*, Uitgave van de universiteit van Leiden.
Lavoie, D. (1987) 'Today's women still face yesterday's values', *Small Business*, 6, 3: 78–80.

Lawrence, J. (1989) *Women in Business – The Problems They Face*, London: Department of Employment, The Training Agency.
Leighton, P. and Felstead, A. (eds) (1992) *The New Entrepreneurs: Self-Employment and Small Business in Europe*, London: Kogan Page.
Lessem, R. (1985) *The Roots of Excellence*, London: Fontana.
—— (1986) *Enterprise Development*, London: Gower Publishing Co.
Lewis, B.C. (1976) 'The limitations of group action among entrepreneurs: the market women of Abidjan, Ivory Coast', in N. J. Hafkin and E. G. Bay (eds) *Women in Africa*, California: Stanford University Press.
Loutfi, M. (1992) 'An overview of self-employment in Europe: nature, trends and policy issues', in P. Leighton and A. Felstead (eds) *The New Entrepreneurs: Self-Employment and Small Business in Europe*, London: Kogan Page.
MacEwen Scott, A. (1979) 'Who are the self employed?' in R. Bromley and C. Gerry (eds) *Casual Work and Poverty in Third World Cities*, Chichester: John Wiley & Son.
Mahon, D. (1973) *No Place in The Country: A Report on Second Homes in England and Wales*, London: Shelter.
Mandl, P.E. (1980) 'Introduction: some facts and figures', in *Assignment Children*, 49/50: 17–41.
Marshall, J. (1984) *Women Managers: Travellers in a Male World*, London: Wiley.
Martin, J. and Roberts, C. (1984) *Women and Employment. A Lifetime Perspective*, London: HMSO.
McColl, J. (1989) 'The value of the awareness campaign as a tool for stimulating enterprise among women', unpublished M.Sc. dissertation, University of Stirling.
Midland Poultry Holdings (1984) *J. P. Wood of Shropshire: 150 Years*, Craven Arms: Midland Poultry.
Mintz, S.W. (1964) 'The employment of capital by market women in Haiti', in R. Firth and B.S. Yamey (eds) *Capital, Saving and Credit in Peasant Societies*, London: George Allen & Unwin Ltd.
Naveed-i-Rahat (1990) 'Male outmigration and matriweighted families: Meharabad, a Punjabi village in Pakistan', in C. M. Cottam-Ellis and S. Rao (eds) *Women, Aid and Development*, Delhi: Hindustan Publishing Corporation.
Nelson, N. (1979) *Why has Development neglected Rural Women?* Oxford: Pergamon Press.
Noble, B.R. (1986) 'Women entrepreneurs, the new business owners', *Venture* July, Part 7: 33–6.
Northern Ireland Equal Opportunities Commission (1987) *Gender Differentiation in Infant Classes*, Belfast: HMSO.
Oakley, A. (1982) *Subject Women*, London: Fontana.
Office of Population Censuses and Surveys (OPCS) (1990) *Population Trends*, Summer, 60: 28—9.
Pahl, R.E. (ed) (1988) *On Work*, Oxford: Basil Blackwell.
Peereboom, E. (ed) (1988) *Werken met MANS*, Utrecht/Antwerpen: Veen.
Peters, T.J. and Waterman, R.G. (1982) *In Search of Excellence*, New York: Harper & Row.

Phizacklea, A. (1988) 'Entrepreneurship, ethnicity and gender', in S. Westwood and P. Bhachu (eds) *Enterprising Women*, London: Routledge.
Pietilä, H. and Vickers, J. (1990) *Making Women Matter: The Role of the United Nations*, London: Zed Books.
Pinchot, G. (1985) *Intrapreneuring*, New York: Harper & Row Publishing Inc.
Poland, F. (1992) 'Trading relationships: house selling and petty enterprise in women's lives', in P. Leighton and A. Felstead (eds) *The New Entrepreneurs: Self-Employment and Small Business in Europe*, London: Kogan Page.
Pollert, A. (1988) 'The "flexible" firm: fixation or fact', *Work Employment and Society* Vol. 2, September: 281–316.
—— (ed.) (1991) *Farewell to Flexibility?* Oxford: Basil Blackwell.
Project Full Employ (1985) Annual Report, London: Project Full Employ.
Rainnie, A. (1989) *Industrial Relations in Small Firms: Small isn't Beautiful*, London: Routledge.
—— (1990) 'Small firms: between the enterprise culture and "new times"', in R. Burrows (ed.) *Deciphering the Enterprise Culture: Entrepreneurship, Petty Capitalism and the Restructuring of Britain*, London: Routledge.
Rajan, A. and Pearson, R. (1986) *UK Occupation and Employment Trends to 1990*, London: Butterworths.
Redclift, N. and Mingione, E. (eds) (1985) *Beyond Employment*, Oxford: Basil Blackwell.
Rees, H. and Shah, A. (1986) 'An empirical analysis of self-employment in the UK', *Journal of Applied Econometrics* 1: 95–108.
Rice, C. and Patel, B. (1988) *Last Among Equals*, Birmingham: West Midlands Low Pay Unit.
Roberts, H. (ed) (1981) *Doing Feminist Research*, London: Routledge & Kegan Paul.
Rosenkrantz, P., Vogel, S., Bee, H., Broverman, J. and Broverman, D. (1968) 'Sex-role stereotypes and self-concept in college students', *Journal of Consulting and Clinical Psychology* 32: 287–95.
Rural Development Commission (1988) 'Promoting jobs and communities in rural England', *Annual Report 1987–1988*.
Sabel, C. (1982) *Work and Politics*, Cambridge: Cambridge University Press.
Saidi, K. (1988) 'Small business credit for Sambura women's groups in Kenya', *Rural Development in Practice* 1, 1: 9–19.
Salisbury, R.F. (1970) *Vunamani – Economic Transformation in a Traditional Society*, Berkeley: University of California Press.
Scase, R. and Goffee, R. (1982) *The Entrepreneurial Middle Class*, London: Croom Helm.
Schreier, J. (1973) *The Female Entrepreneur: A Pilot Study*, Milwaukee, Wis.: Center for Venture Management.
Schutt, J. and Whittington, R. (1984) 'Large firms and the rise of small units', Nottingham: Small Firms Research Conference. Mimeo.
Schwartz, E.B. (1976) 'Entrepreneurship: a new female frontier', *Journal of Contemporary Business* 5, Winter: 47–76.
Scott, S. (1985) 'Feminist research and qualitative methods', in R. Burgess (ed.) *Issues in Educational Research: Qualitative Methods*, Lewes: Falmer Press.

Bibliography 169

Shakeshaft, C. and Nowell, I. (1984) 'Research on themes, concepts and models of organisational behaviour: the influence of gender', in *Issues in Education* 2, 3: 186–203.

Shropshire County Council (1983) '1981 Census', *Small Area Statistics*, Shrewsbury: Shropshire County Council.

Sivard, R.L. (1985) *Women . . . A World Survey*, Washington: World Priorities.

SKIM (Statistisch Kwalitatie Industrieel Marktonderzoek) (1985) *Door vrouwen opgerichte bedrijven*, Den Haag.

SKIM/EIM (Statistisch Kwalitatie Industrieel Marktonderzoek/Economisch Instituut voor het Midden en Kleinbedrijf) (1988) *Vrouwelijke ondernemers: ondernemerschap, ondersteuningsbehoeften en ondersteuningsaanbod*, Rotterdam: Ministeries van Economische Zaken en Sociale Zaken en Werkgelegenheid.

Skinner, L. (1989) *Small Business Start up Training for Women. A report for the Training Agency*, University of Bristol: Business Development Centre.

Small Business Administration (1985) 'The state of small business: a report to the President', Washington DC: United States Government Printing Office.

Soloman, G.T. and Fernald, L.W. (1988) 'Value profiles of male and female entrepreneurs', *International Small Business Journal*, 6, 3: 24–33.

Stevenson, L. (1983) 'An investigation into the entrepreneurial experience of women', *ASAC Proceedings* Vancouver: University of British Columbia.

Sym, L. and Lewis, J. (1987) *Education Needs of Small Business Start-Ups. An Investigation of Short Course Provision*, Paper presented at the 10th National Small Firms Policy and Research Conference, Milton Keynes.

Telford Development Corporation (1990) *Telford Workforce: Key Facts for Employers prepared for Telford Development Corporation*, Telford: TDC Market Research Section and Prism Research Ltd, May.

Toffler, A. (1980) *The Third Wave*, London: Collins/Pan Books.

Truman, C. (1989) Good practice in local enterprise agencies', London: Report to Business in the Community

Turner, C. (1989) 'Sources of support for women's LEIs in the European Community', Brussels: Commission of the European Communities.

—— (1990) 'Sectoral and regional analysis of women's LEIs in the EEC', Brussels: Report for the Commission of the European Communities.

Turner, C. and Papioannou, V. (1988) Women's local employment initiatives in Greece', Brussels: Report for the Commission of the European Communities.

United States Small Business Administration (1985) *The State of Small Business 1985*, Washington: United States Small Business Administration.

van der Wees, C., and Romijn, H. (1987) 'Entrepreneurship and small enterprise development for women in developing countries: an agenda of unanswered questions', Geneva: Management Development Programme, ILO.

van Eijndhoven, M. (1986) 'Vrouwen ondernemen, waarom niet?' *Kroniek van het Ambacht/Klein- en Middenbedrijf* 2: 37–9.

van Vianen, A.E.M., van Schie, E.C.M. and Willems, T.M. (1986) *Werving en Selectie. De behandeling van vrouwen en mannen*, Universiteit te Leiden: Werkgroep Arbeidsvraagstukken en Welzijn.

Veenstra, T. (1986) *Zippen vrouwen weer te zeuren? Erzaringen van onderneemsters met het fenomeen instanties*, Tilburg: University of Tilburg.

Watkins, D.S. and Watkins, J. (1982) 'The female entrepreneur – American experience and its implications for the UK', in J. Stanworth, A. Westrip, D. Watkins, J. Lewis (eds) *Perspectives on a Decade of Small Business Research*, Aldershot: Gower.

—— (1984) 'The female entrepreneur: her background and determinants of business choice, some British data', *International Small Business Journal*, 2, 4: 21–31.

Wegner, D.M. and Vallacher, R.P. (1977) *Implicit Psychology: An Introduction to Social Cognition*, New York: Oxford University Press.

Weiner, M. (1981) *English Culture and the Decline of the Industrial Spirit 1850–1980*, Cambridge: Cambridge University Press.

West Midlands Enterprise Board (WMEB) (1986) *Sector Review: Clothing Industry*, Birmingham: West Midlands Enterprise Board.

—— (1988) *Sector Review: Clothing Industry*, Birmingham: West Midlands Enterprise Board.

Whitmont, E.C. (1983) *Return of the Goddess*, London: RKP.

Williams, S. (1985) *A Job to Live: The Impact of Tomorrow's Technology on Work and Society*, London: Penguin.

Women's World Bank (1987) Personal communication, December 10.

Young, M. and Willmott, P. (1973) *The Symmetrical Family*, London: Routledge & Kegan Paul.

Author index

Ahmed, A. S. and Ahmed, Z. 22
Allen, S. 34, 88
Allen, S. et al. 7
Allen, S. and Truman, C. 2, 3, 12, 88, 149, 160; typology of entrepreneurs 153
Allen, S. and Wolkowitz, C. 2, 6, 7
Amsterdam-Rotterdam Bank 69
Andersen, V. 94, 95, 98
Atkinson, J. 7
Bangun, M. 16, 19
Barron, K. J. and Norris, G. M. 94
Bernard, J. 158
Birmingham Women's Enterprise Development Agency 44
Boulgarides, J. D. 47
Boyer, R. 7
Broadley, C. J. 89, 94, 98
Bromley, R. and Gerry, C. 6
Brown, P. and Scase, R. 7
Burke, W. W. 47
Burr, R. 34
Burrows, R. and Curran, J. 6, 7
Business in the Community 121

Cannon, T. et al. 95, 99, 159
Carr, M. 19, 20–1
Carter, S. and Cannon, T. 33, 71, 149, 151, 153; experience 103; female employees 81; high achievers 90–1; motivations 154; problems 41, 154–5; returners 89–90; start-up training 95
Carter, S. et al. 149
Casey, B. and Creigh, S. 2
Cassidy, R. 18
Castillo, G. T. 16

Central Bureau voor de Statistiek (CBS) 57
Chaganti, R. 53
Chan Shui-Ying, L. 99, 100
Clutterbuck, D. and Devine, M. 48, 49, 50, 56
Collom, D. 150
Commission of European Communities 134
Cottam, C. M. 22
Creigh, S. et al. 32, 70, 71, 72, 73
Cromie, S. and Hayes, J. 149, 152
Cuba, R. et al. 47
Cunningham, I. 49
Curran, J. 148, 149, 152, 159; enterprise climate 86; family of origin 33; sample sizes 154, 157
Curran, J. and Burrows, R. 70, 71, 72, 76, 160
Curran, J. and Stanworth, J. 94, 95
Curran, J. et al. 160

Daune-Richard, A. M. 7
Davidson, M. and Cooper, C. 94
Davies, R. 6
De Rijk, C. G. H. 58
Delamont, S. 28
Department of Employment 30, 86, 104, 107, 148, 156
Devine, M. and Clutterbuck, D. 56
Dhamija, J. 19
Drucker, P. 53, 147

EEC 3
Elson, D. and Pearson, R. 6
Emler, N. and Abrams, D. 59
Employment Gazette 86, 87
EOC 129

Women in business

Epstein, T. S. 16, 18, 26
Fevre, R. 7
Food and Agriculture Organization 16, 23
Galbraith, J. K. 29
Ganguly, P. 73, 85, 148
Gerry, C. 7
Gershuny, J. I. 6
Gershuny, J. I. and Pahl, R. E. 6
Goffee, R. and Scase, R. 47, 71, 149, 151, 154; family support 98; typology of entrepreneurs 90, 152-3
Goffee, R. et al. 151
Goldstein, N. 93
Goldthorpe, J. H. 33
Government White Paper 86, 87

Haas, L. and Nesemann, C. 134
Hakim, C. 100, 104
Halpern, M. and Szurek, J. C. 89, 90, 100, 134, 144
Hamilton, D. 151
Hampson, A. 61
Handy, C. 49
Hayden, C. 102
Hertz, L. 34, 48, 56
Hill, P. 22
Hisrich, R. and Brush, C. 89, 95, 149, 150, 155
Hobbs, D. 1
Holmquist, C. and Sundin, E. 90
Howieson, C. 134
Hughey, A. and Gelman, E. 67
Hunt, A. 70
Hymounts, C. 90

Iglesias, G. U. 22
Illo, J. F. 22

Jenson, J. et al. 6
Jones, M. 42
Josefowitz, N. 50
Joss, S. 24

Kaur, D. and Hayden, C. 102
Knight, G. and Taylor, A. 15-16
Koopman, A. C. and Walvis, C. 59, 61
Koper, G. and Vermunt, R. 57, 60

Lavoie, D. 150
Lawrence, J. 94
Leighton, P. and Felstead, A. 1, 3
Lessem, R. 50, 52
Lewis, B. C. 23
Loutfi, M. 2

MacEwen Scott, A. 6
Mahon, D. 29
Mandl, P. E. 21, 23-4
Marshall, J. 47
Martin, J. and Roberts, C. 88
McColl, J. 94
Midland Poultry Holdings 31
Mintz, S. W. 16, 17, 17-18

Naveed-i-Rahat 22
Nelson, N. 14
Noble, B. R. 51
Northern Ireland EOC 93

Oakley, A. 94
Office of Population Censuses and Surveys 29

Pahl, R. E. 6
Peereboom, E. 67
Peters, T. J. and Waterman, R. G. 67
Phizacklea, A. 102
Pietilä, H. and Vickers, J. 13
Pinchot, G. 50
Poland, F. 6
Pollert, A. 7

Rainnie, A. 7
Rajan, A. and Pearson, R. 85
Redclift, N. and Mingione, E. 6
Rees, H. and Shah, A. 151
Rice, C. and Patel, B. 104
Roberts, H. 159
Rosenkrantz, P. et al. 61
Rural Development Commission 29

Sabel, C. 7
Saidi, K. 24
Salisbury, R. F. 18
Scase, R. and Goffee, R. 160
Schreier, J. 149, 150
Schutt, J. and Whittington, R. 7
Schwartz, E. B. 149, 150
Scott, S. 158

Shakeshaft, C. and Nowell, I. 151
Shropshire County Council 32
Sivard, R. L. 24
SKIM/EIM 69
Skinner, L. 89, 99
Small Business Administration 156
Solomon, G. T. and Fernald, L. W. 149
Statistisch Kwalitatie Industrieel Marktonderzoek (SKIM) 59, 60
Stevenson, L. 149, 151, 155
Sym, L. and Lewis, J. 97

Telford Development Corporation 30
Toffler, A. 6
Truman, C. 5
Turner, C. 134, 135, 137, 141, 144
Turner, C. and Papioannou, V. 134

Van der Wees, C. and Romijn, H. 148, 156
Van Eijndhoven, M. 69
Van Vianen, A. E. M. et al. 65
Veenstra, T. 59

Watkins, D. S. and Watkins, J. 33, 48, 71, 76, 149, 152
Wegner, D. M. and Vallacher, R. P. 61
Weiner, M. 148
Welsh Language Society 29
West Midlands Enterprise Board 102
Whitmont, E. C. 49
Williams, S. 148
Women's World Bank 25

Young, M. and Willmott, P. 39

Subject index

Aberdeen Enterprise Trust 99–100
accountancy training 26
active learning 97
ADIEF 143
advice: difficulty of obtaining 103–4;
 LEAs 126–7; need for specialist
 106–7, 108, 109, 112, 115–16, 119–
 20; *see also* advice/support
 agencies; support
advice/support agencies 11, 99, 119;
 EC 137–9; lack of understanding
 for women 103–4, 131–2; start-ups
 91, 92; typology of 131; women's
 127; *see also* local enterprise
 agencies
advocacy 128
affirmative action (AA) 58, 67
age: small business owners 71–2, 75,
 76; structure of rural population
 30
agriculture 13, 15, 15–16
androcentrism 151
awareness-creation 139, 141, 142

banks: discrimination by 13, 54, 103,
 119–20, 141–2; Netherlands and
 credit 9–10, 59–69; problems with
 40, 103, 128; start-up finance from
 76–8; training needed for staff 142
barriers 8, 150–1, 152, 155; *see also*
 credit; finance; sectoral
 segregation
Bastardo, Josephina 25
Bathgate Area Support for
 Enterprise (BASE) Ltd 91–3, 95,
 96–7, 98–9, 100
Black Country Fashions 117–18

bleeding Madras 19
Bothakga Handknits 20
Botswana 26
Bristol study 48–56; advice to other
 women entrepreneurs 54–5;
 comments on being female 54;
 comments on management 55–6;
 follow-up 54; management styles
 52–3; motivators 49–50; previous
 experience 50–1; qualities and
 strengths 51
Britain: research into female
 entrepreneurship 151–6; self-
 employment 2–3, 30, 70, 88–9,
 134, 148
Bugden, Rosemary 49, 50
bundles, sales in 18
Burt, Sue 49, 50, 52, 53, 54, 56
business clubs 92, 98, 118, 128–9
Business in the Community 31
business enterprise, classifying 2–4
business growth 43, 155; *see also*
 expansion business information/
 advice services *see* advice/support
 agencies; local enterprise agencies
business ownership: dynamic process
 153–4; increase by women 88–9;
 problems 154–5; *see also*
 entrepreneurship; self-
 employment; small business sector
business plans; assistance with 111,
 119, 125; banks and 63, 65–6, 128
business skills 95, 139; courses 108–
 10, 111; *see also* management style

capital: shortage 23; substitution of

labour for 15, 17; see also credit; finance
caring management style 52-3
challenge, as motivator 50
children 37-8, 43, 64, 68; see also domestic/family responsibilities; family
clothing industry see West Midlands Clothing
collateral 13, 23, 95-6, 103, 141; see also credit
community groups/organizations 124, 125
conventional entrepreneurs 90, 152
Coode, Sally Jane 49, 51, 52
cooked food 18-19
cooperative management 52-3
cooperatives, marketing 19, 117-18
Council for Small Industries in Rural Areas 29
counselling 91; LEAs 121, 126-7; see also advice; support
credit; entry barrier 8; incentive programme 67-9; need for research 12-13; Netherlands study see credit-granting study; petty entrepreneurs 15-16, 23, 24-5; start-up training 95-6; see also finance
credit-granting study (Netherlands) 9-10, 59-66; entrepreneurs' perceptions 62, 65-6; objective aspects 60-1; research findings 63-5; subjective aspects 61-2
cultural norms 22

data collection 156, 158-9
decision making 51; as motivator 50; unpalatable and expansion 55
Designer Show-Case Boutique 117-18
Development Commission 29
discontinuous career pattern 60
discrimination 101, 119-20; banks/financial institutions 13, 54, 103, 119-20, 141-2; EAS 87-8, 100, 103; qualitative research techniques 158; race and gender 106
dissatisfaction, as motivator 49

domestic entrepreneurs 153
domestic/family responsibilities 9, 86, 130; business skills learned from 95, 139; 'conventional' entrepreneurs 90; credit requests 64; gender relations 12; Netherlands 59, 64, 68; role conflict 151; rural women 38-40; separation of training from 10-11, 96; Third World women 15, 22, 23; see also multiple roles
domestic technologies 15, 24, 39

economic change 4-8
Economic Development Units (EDUs) 92, 108
education: limitation of low levels 23-4; Netherlands 59, 67; qualifications 36, 42-3, 71, 76, 77; rural women 35-6; see also training
employee relations 155
employment in small businesses 79, 80, 80-1, 82, 83-4
Employment Training (ET) 87, 95
enabling management style 52-3
Enterprise Allowance Scheme (EAS) 87, 92, 103, 119; discrimination against women 87-8, 100, 103; survival rate 107-8; women participants 89
enterprise agencies see advice/support agencies; local enterprise agencies
enterprise culture 6-7, 86-8, 147
Enterprise in Higher Education 87
Enterprise Training 87
enterprises, classifying 2-4
entrepreneurial ideals 152-3
entrepreneurial ideology 5
entrepreneurship: characteristics associated with 59, 61, 63, 64-5, 66, 67-8; growth in female in EC 133-4; historical perspective 5; motivations for see motivations; qualities and strengths of female 51; self-employment and 70; types of in the Third World 15-21; typology of female 152-3; see also

Women in business

business ownership; self-employment
equal opportunities 47, 144, 145
equality in management 52–3
European Community (EC) 11, 133–47; Equal Opportunities Programmes 144, 145; Equal Treatment Directive 58; growth in female entrepreneurship 133–4; growth in self-employment 2–3, 134; motivations for self-employment 135–6; programme for women's employment initiatives 143–6; sectoral trends 134–5; support 136–43, 147
European Community grants 92, 144–5, 146
European Network for Women in Local Employment Initiatives 145–6
expansion, business 55; constraints on petty entrepreneurs 23–4; *see also* business growth
experience 36, 59; Bristol study 50–1; comparative study 71, 76, 77; lack and sectoral choice 152; transferring skills from domestic work 95, 139
exports 16
extended family 23

fabric wholesalers 116–17
failure rate 85
family: 'new work collective' 6; of origin and self-employment 33–5; support from 37–8, 98; *see also* children
family responsibilities *see* domestic/family responsibilites
fast moving consumer goods (FMCG) 107
female-headed households 21
finance: EC 92, 141–3, 144–5; entry barrier 103, 106, 155; sources for start-up 76–8, 92; West Midlands Clothing Project 108, 109, 114–15; *see also* banks; credit; financial institutions
financial institutions 13, 119–20,
142; EC 141–2; *see also* banks; credit
fish smoking 19
flexible specialization 7
food; trading 18–19; women's role in production 2, 13
frame of reference, missing 61, 68
France 145; government loan guarantee scheme 142, 143

gender 1–2; comparison of business owners 10, 70–85; income differential 21–2; inequalities in the Netherlands 57–8; lack of autonomy and self-employment 12; management style and 47–8; roles and typology of female entrepreneurs 152–3; West Midlands Clothing Project 105–6, 113–14
gender division of labour 23–4, 64; *see also* domestic/family responsibilities; sectoral segregation
gender-related problems 40–1, 154–5, 156
Germany 134
Ghana 19
'glass-ceiling' effect 90–1
Goldrausch 142
Gordon, Daphne 51
Greece, 134, 145
Greenleaf co-operatives 51, 53

Haiti 16, 17–18
handicrafts 19
Heaton, Brinion 54
Henning, Peggy 47
Hickling, Dee 51, 54
higglers, 15–16, 31
honour, concept of 22
household responsibilities *see* domestic/family responsibilities
husbands/partners: stability of relationship 43; support from 37–8

IBIS 98
Ibu Sai 18–19
imports 16
incentive programme for credit-granting 67–9

income differential 21-2
independence 154
India 11, 19, 22, 147
Indonesia 16
Industrial Revolution 28
innovation 134-5
innovative entrepreneurs 152-3
Instant Muscle 87, 92
international division of labour 7
interviews, personal 158

Jamaican higglers 15-16
joint marketing venture 117-18
Judy's Fruits 25

Kaur, Davinder 110
Kaur, Jagdeep 115
Kenya 9, 16, 20
Kidstuff 49, 50, 53
King, Delores 115
Knight, Shirley 52

labour, substitution of for capital 15, 17
labour market: changes in 1980s 5-6; difficulties in access 136; sociology of 6; status by race and gender in West Midlands 105-6; support agencies' perception 131-2; women's participation in the Netherlands 57-8; women's self-employment and 160
Liberia 22
Lijjat Pappad 19
Livewire 87, 92
Lloyd, Caroline 51, 54
loan guarantee scheme, France 142
local enterprise agencies (LEAs) 121-32; business clubs 128-9; content and quality of counselling and advice 126-7; limits to influence 130-2; marketing services to women 124-5; monitoring information 122-4; outreach work 125-6; perceptions of women and labour market 131-2; provision of training 129-30; small business support networks 121-2; special events 126; support and advocacy 128; women as clients 122

location-specific resource and market surveys 26

Major, John 1
make-through clothing sector 106-7
management skills, home-learned 95, 139
management style 9, 46-8, 56; Bristol study 52-3, 55-6; changing and expansion 55; human-interest oriented 67; research into female 47-8
management training 26, 55-6, 56
marital relationship see husbands/ partners
market gap, as motivator 49
marketing: advice 108, 109; clothing sector 107, 108, 109; co-operatives 19, 117-18; gender-related problems 40-1; LEAs' services to women 124-5; petty entrepreneurs' restrictions 24, 26
mechanization, rural 21, 28
Melanesia 18
Merbial Valley (Haiti) 17-18
methodological problems in research 156-60; data collection 158-9; sample size 154, 157-8, 159; theoretical framework 159-60
Mexico 18
micro-business 3; see also small business sector
Midland Poultry Holdings 31
migration, rural-urban 28-30
Miller, Diane 49, 50
Minerva matrix 48-9; see also Bristol study
monitoring information, LEAs and 122-4
motivations for entrepreneurship 89-91, 135-6; Bristol study 49-50; research 149, 150, 154, 156; Third World women 14
Mraru bus service (Kenya) 20
mulberry trees 26
multiple roles 14-15, 28, 38-40; see also domestic/family responsibilities
Muslim societies 22

Netherlands, The 57-69; credit study

60–6; incentive credit programme 67–9; support funding 142; women entrepreneurs 58–60; women in labour market 57–8
networks: EC 143, 145–6; rural women 41–2; start-up training 95, 98–9; West Midlands Clothing Project 109, 118; *see also* local enterprise agencies; support
North American research 150–1 *see also* United States

Occupations Study Group (OSG) surveys 72–85; changes between 1985 and 1988 82–4; characteristics of businesses in 1985 79–82; start-up process 75–9
Okobank 142
outreach work 125–6, 138–9
Overton, Jane 31

Paisley Enterprise Trust 100
Pakistan 13, 22
Papua New Guinea 16, 18
parental support 37
partners *see* husbands/partners
partnership training 129
part-time work 69, 90; Netherlands 57, 64; self-employment as alternative to low-paid 102, 105
Pearson, Jennifer Bryant 54
personal development 43–4, 53, 94
personal interviews 158
petty female entrepreneurs 14–27; constraints preventing expansion 23–4; constraints on rural women 21–3; multiple roles 14–15; policy changes necessary 24–6; types of entrepreneurship 15–21
Philippines 16, 22
Pinto, Frances 56
'pioneer approach' 50–1
Portugal 144–5, 145
post-Fordism 7
poverty, as motivator 14
press coverage 124
Prince's Youth Business Trust 87
problems: comparative study 78–9; gender-related 40–1, 154–5, 156; Third World rural women 21–4
production management advice 109

profitability: comparative study 79, 80, 83, 84; credit and 60, 63
promotional material 124–5
Pukhtun society (Pakistan) 22
purdah 22

qualifications, educational 36, 42–3, 71, 76, 77
qualitative research techniques 158–9
Queen Margaret College, Edinburgh 100

race, Clothes Project and 104, 104–6, 113–14
radical entrepreneurs 153
research 7–8, 12, 71–2, 148–60; British 151–6; methodological problems 156–60; North American 150–1
restructuring 5–7
returners 89–90
role conflict 151
Rural Development Commission 29, 31
Rural Industries Bureau 29
rural–urban migration 28–30
rural women 9; multiple roles 14–15, 28, 38–40; Shropshire *see* South Shropshire study; Third World *see* petty female entrepreneurs

Sabrina Vallis 49, 50, 53, 54
sample sizes 145, 156, 157–8, 159
savings, personal 76, 77
school 35; *see also* education
SCOTEC Technician Certificate in Electrical and Electronic Engineering 93
Scotland 91–100
Scottish Enterprise Foundation (SEF) 91–3, 95, 96–7, 98–9, 100
secondary data sources 159
sectoral segregation 8, 152; comparative study 72, 73–5; Netherlands 57, 60–1, 63–4; petty female entrepreneurs 24
sectoral trends 150, 152; EAS survivors 107; EC women's enterprises 134–5

Subject index 179

Self-Employed Women's Association (SEWA) 11, 147
self-employment 9; barriers in clothing business 102–4; British statistics 2–3, 30, 70, 88–9, 134, 148; EC growth 2–3, 134; and entrepreneurship 70; and labour market 160; lack of autonomy 12; promotion 86–7; South Shropshire study 31–2, 36–7
self-exploitation 9, 12, 131
sericulture 26
service sectors 107; comparative study 73–5; EC women's employment 134; see also sectoral segregation
sex stereotyping 61–2, 64–5
sexual division of labour 23–4, 64
Sheppard, Sue 51
Shirley, Steve 52
Shropshire 30–1; see also South Shropshire study skills 53; business skills learned from homemaking 95, 139; see aslo training
small business sector 3–4; comparative study 70–85; defining 3; enterprise culture in 1980s 6–7; growth 148–9; research 7, 149; start-ups see start-ups; support networks see local enterprise agencies
Smith, Ann 114
social change 4–8
social science 4
social security benefits 68, 126
socialization, differential 34–5, 59
South Shropshire study 31–44; educational qualifications and training 36; family of origin 33–5; family support 37–8; follow-up interviews 42–4; gender-related problems 40–1; multiple roles 38–40; networking and support 41–2; school 35; self-employment 31–2, 36–7
South West Women into Management (SWWIM) 46
Spain 144–5, 145
special events 126

specialization, flexible 7
Squires, Sarah 49, 50, 53
start-up training 10, 91–100; content 94; duration 95–6; process 97–8; support 98–9; timing 96–7
start-ups 10; motivations for see motivations; OSG surveys 75–9; support 91, 92; training see start-up training; West Midlands see West Midlands Clothing
state benefits 68, 126
'statistical' purdah 2
Steen, Gunnilla 50
Strathkelvin Enterprise Trust 99
Sugarcraft 54
support 10–12, 54; EC 136–46, 147; family 37–8, 98; LEAs 128; from other women 41–2; rural women's needs 45; for small business start-ups 91, 92; start-up training 98–9; West Midlands Clothing Project 111–14; see also advice/support agencies; local enterprise agencies; networks survival, as motivator 49

targeted enterprise initiatives 87–8
team-based management 52–3
technical information 109, 111
technical training 140
Technical and Vocational Education Initiatives (TVEI) 87
technology, new 81, 82
Telford 30–1
thematic approach to training 97–8
theoretical framework 156, 159–60
Third World 9, 37; petty entrepreneurs see petty female entrepreneurs
Thompson, Julie 115
time management 38–9, 41, 43
trade links 17
trading 9, 15–18
training 119; for advisers/counsellors 127, 139; comparative study 76, 77; EC and 139–41, 142; for financial institutions' staff 142; LEA provision 129–30; management 26, 55–6, 56; Netherlands women 59, 67; for petty female entrepreneurs 25–6;

separate for women 99, 140; separation from domestic/family responsibilities 10–11, 96; South Shropshire study 36, 42–3; start-up *see* start-up training; West Midlands Clothing Project 108–10, 111–14
Training Agency 92, 99
Training Commission (TC) 129
transformational management 52–3
turnover 78, 79–80, 81, 82, 83, 84

unemployment: EC 135, 143–4; measures to combat 87–8; statistics undercounting women 88; support for start-ups 113; West Midlands 104, 105–6
United States 148; *see also* North American research

Vunapope market (Papua New Guinea) 18

weavers' co-operative 19
West Midlands Clothing Business Start-Up Project 11, 101–20; breaking into clothing business 102–4; Business Club 118; fabric sourcing 116–17; joint marketing 117–18; needs and aims 108–11; new clothing entrepreneurs 104–8; support and training 108–10, 111–14; women working for success 114–16
West Midlands Clothing Resource Centre 101, 102, 110–11, 114–18, 120
Wolverhampton 117–18
women bank employees 68
Women in Enterprise 92, 127
Women into Science and Engineering (WISE) 93
women-only training 99, 140
women's business advice agencies 127
Women's Enterprise Development Agency (WEDA) 92, 127, 137, 138, 140
Women's World Bank (WWB) 25, 137, 140, 142
Wood (J. P.) and Sons 31
word of mouth 124
work, reformulation of 6
work load, Third World women and 24
working mothers/grandmothers 34
Workstart 100